LEVITICUS & DEUTERONOMY

Visions of the Promised Land

John MacArthur

Harper*Christian*
Resources

MacArthur Bible Studies
Leviticus & Deuteronomy: Visions of the Promised Land
© 2022 by John MacArthur

Requests for information should be addressed to:
HarperChristian Resources, 3900 Sparks Dr. SE, Grand Rapids, Michigan 49546

ISBN 978-0-310-12374-3 (softcover)
ISBN 978-0-310-12375-0 (ebook)

HarperChristian Resources titles may be purchased in bulk for church, business, fundraising, or ministry use. For information, please e-mail ResourceSpecialist@ChurchSource.com.

First Printing October 2022 / Printed in the United States of America

CONTENTS

INTRODUCTION

Law and history are the building blocks of a people and culture. The *law* sets the boundaries for a populace in the present moment. *History* tells the people how they arrived at that present moment so they can move forward. *Laws* enable people to know the rules of a society and what is expected of them. History helps people remember what happens when those rules are not followed so they are not doomed to repeat those past mistakes.

The Israelites' exodus from the land of Egypt marked the end of a period of oppression in their history. It also constituted the beginning of the fulfillment of God's covenantal promise to Abraham that his descendants would not only reside in the Promised Land but would also multiply and become a great nation (see Genesis 12:1–3, 7). So, at appropriate times—on Mount Sinai and in the plains of Moab—God gave the people of Israel a body of legislation, the *law*, to instruct them on how to live properly as the theocratic people of God. By this, the Israelites were to be distinct from all other nations on earth (see Deuteronomy 4:7–8).

In this study, we will explore the laws that God gave to His people as recorded in the books of Leviticus and Deuteronomy. As we do so, we will see the incredible lengths to which God went to stress the critical importance of personal holiness to His people at the very beginning of their journey. We will also see how Moses, at the end of his life, desperately called that same people to reject the mistakes that they had made in their history and choose a better future—one of *life* rather than *death,* and *blessing* rather than *curse.*

THE BOOK OF LEVITICUS

The original Hebrew title of this third book of the law is taken from its first word, translated "and He called." Several Old Testament books derive their Hebrew names in the same manner (for example, Genesis, "in the beginning," and Exodus, "now these are the names"). The English title *Leviticus* comes from the Latin Vulgate version of the Greek Old Testament (LXX), *Levitikon*, meaning "matters of the Levites" (see Leviticus 25:32–33). While the book addresses issues regarding the Levites' responsibilities, more significantly, it instructs all the priests in how they are to assist the people in worship and how the people are to lead holy lives before God. New Testament writers quote the book of Leviticus more than fifteen times.

AUTHOR AND DATE

Authorship and date issues are resolved by the concluding verse of the book: "These are the commandments which the LORD commanded Moses for the children of Israel on Mount Sinai" (27:34). The fact that God gave these laws to Moses (see, for example, 1:1) appears fifty-six times in the book. In addition to recording detailed prescriptions, Leviticus chronicles several historical accounts relating to the laws (see 8:1–10:20; 24:10–23). Regarding the date of the book, the Exodus occurred in 1445 BC, and the tabernacle was finished one year later. Leviticus picks up the record at that point, likely revealed in the first month (Abib/Nisan) of the second year after the Exodus. Numbers begins after that, in the second month (see Numbers 1:1).

BACKGROUND AND SETTING

Before the year that Israel camped at Mount Sinai, the presence of God's glory had never formally resided among the Israelites. A central place of worship, like the tabernacle, had never existed, nor had a structured and regulated set of sacrifices and feasts been given. Furthermore, the office of a high priest, the formal priesthood, and a cadre of tabernacle workers had not yet been appointed. As the book of Exodus concludes, the tabernacle has been completed, requiring there to now be structured sacrifices, feasts, and established roles for the priesthood and tabernacle workers. This is what the book of Leviticus provides.

The Lord had called Israel to be "a kingdom of priests and a holy nation" (Exodus 19:6). Up to this point, Israel had only the historical records of the patriarchs from which to gain their knowledge of how to worship and live before their God. Having been slaves for centuries in Egypt, the land of a seemingly infinite number of gods, their concept of worship and godly living was severely distorted. Their tendency to hold on to polytheism and pagan ritual is witnessed in the wilderness wanderings (see Exodus 32). God would not permit them to worship in the ways of their Egyptian neighbors, nor would He tolerate Egyptian ideas about morality and sin. The instructions in Leviticus enabled the priests to lead Israel in worship appropriate to the Lord.

Even though the book of Leviticus contains a great deal of law, it is presented in a narrative format. Immediately after Moses supervised the construction of the tabernacle, God came in glory to dwell there. This marked the close of the book of Exodus (see 40:34–38). Leviticus begins with God calling Moses from the tabernacle and ends with God's commands to Moses in the form of binding legislation. Israel's King had occupied His palace (the tabernacle), instituted His law, and declared Himself a covenant partner with His subjects. No geographical movement occurs in this book. The people stay at the foot of Mount Sinai, where God came down to give His law. They were still there one month later when the record of Numbers begins.

HISTORICAL AND THEOLOGICAL THEMES

The core ideas around which Leviticus develops are the holy character of God and His will for Israel's holiness. The Lord's holiness, mankind's sinfulness, sacrifice, and God's presence in the sanctuary are the book's most common themes. The book sets forth instruction, in a clear and authoritative tone, about personal holiness (see, for example, 11:44, 45; 19:2; 20:7, 26). Matters pertaining to Israel's life of faith tend to focus on purity in ritual settings, but not to the exclusion of concerns regarding Israel's personal purity. In fact, there is a continuing emphasis on personal holiness in response to the holiness of God (emphasized especially in chapters 17–27). On more than 125 occasions, Leviticus indicts mankind for uncleanness and/or instructs on how to be purified. The motive for such holiness is stated in two repeated phrases: "I am the LORD," and, "I am holy."

The theme of the conditional Mosaic Covenant resurfaces throughout the book, but particularly in chapter 26. This contract for the new nation not only details the consequences for obedience or disobedience to the covenant stipulations, it does so in a manner scripted for determining Israel's history. One cannot help but recognize prophetic implications in the punishments for disobedience, as they sound like the events of the much later Babylonian deportment, captivity, and subsequent return to the land (c. 538 BC), which occurred almost 900 years after Moses wrote Leviticus. The eschatological implications for Israel's disobedience will not conclude until Messiah comes to introduce His kingdom and end the curses of Leviticus 26 and Deuteronomy 28 (see Zechariah 14:11).

The five sacrifices and offerings mentioned in the book were symbolic, designed to allow the truly penitent and thankful worshiper to express faith in and love for God by the observance of these rituals. When the worshiper's heart was not penitent and thankful, God was not pleased with the ritual. The offerings were burnt, symbolizing the worshiper's desire to be purged of sin and sending up the fragrant smoke of true worship to God. The myriad of small details in the execution of the rituals is intended to teach exactness and precision that would extend to the way the people obeyed the moral and spiritual laws of God and the way they revered every facet of His Word.

INTERPRETIVE CHALLENGES

Leviticus is both a manual for the worship of God in Israel and a theology of old covenant ritual. Understanding the ceremonies, laws, and ritual details prescribed in the book is difficult today because Moses assumed a certain context of historical understanding. Once the challenge of understanding the detailed prescriptions has been met, the question arises as to how believers in the church should respond to them, since the New Testament clearly abrogates Old Testament ceremonial law (see Acts 10:1–16; Colossians 2:16–17), the Levitical priesthood (see 1 Peter 2:9; Revelation 1:6; 5:10; 20:6), and the sanctuary (see Matthew 27:51), as well as instituting the New Covenant (see Matthew 26:28; 2 Corinthians 3:6–18; Hebrews 7–10).

Rather than try to practice the old ceremonies or look for some deeper spiritual significance in them, the focus for the reader should be on the holy and divine character behind them. This may partly be the reason why certain explanations that Moses gave in the prescriptions for cleanness offer greater insight into the mind of God than do the ceremonies themselves. The spiritual principles in which the rituals are rooted are timeless because they are embedded in the nature of God. The New Testament makes it clear that from Pentecost forward the church is under the authority of the New Covenant, not the old covenant.

There is often a desire among interpreters to compare features of this book with New Testament writers who present types or analogies based on the tabernacle and the ceremonial aspects of the law to teach lessons about Christ and New-Covenant reality. Although the ceremonial law served as a shadow of the reality of Christ and His redemptive work (see Hebrews 10:1), excessive typology is to be rejected. Only that which New Testament writers identify as types of Christ should be so designated (see, for example, 1 Corinthians 5:7).

The most profitable study in Leviticus is thus that which yields truth in the understanding of sin, guilt, substitutionary death, and atonement by focusing on features that are not explained or illustrated elsewhere in the Old Testament. Later Old Testament authors, and especially New Testament writers, built on the basic understanding of these matters provided in Leviticus. The sacrificial features of Leviticus point to their ultimate, one-time fulfillment in the substitutionary death of Jesus Christ (see Hebrews 9:11–22).

THE BOOK OF DEUTERONOMY

The English title *Deuteronomy* comes from the Greek Septuagint (LXX) mistranslation of "copy of this law" in 17:18 as "second law," which was rendered *Deuteronomium* in the Latin version (Vulgate). The Hebrew title of the book is translated, "These are the words," from the first two Hebrew words of the book. In truth, this is a better description of the book, since it is not a "second law" but rather the record of Moses' words of explanation concerning the law. Deuteronomy completes the five-part literary unit known as the Pentateuch, that begins with Genesis.

AUTHOR AND DATE

Moses has traditionally been recognized as the author of Deuteronomy, as the book itself testifies that he wrote it (see 1:1, 5; 31:9, 22, 24). Both the Old Testament and the New Testament support this claim (see 1 Kings 2:3; 8:53; 2 Kings 14:6; 18:12; Acts 3:22–23; Romans 10:19). Although Deuteronomy 32:48–34:12 was added after Moses' death (probably by Joshua), the rest of the book came from Moses' hand, just before his death in 1405 BC.

The majority of the book is comprised of farewell speeches that the 120-year-old Moses gave to the Israelites, beginning on the first day of the eleventh month of the fortieth year after the Exodus from Egypt (see Deuteronomy 1:3). These speeches can be dated January–February of 1405 BC. In the last few weeks of Moses' life, he committed these speeches to writing and gave them to the priests and elders for the coming generations of Israel (see 31:9, 24–26).

BACKGROUND AND SETTING

Deuteronomy, like Leviticus, takes place entirely in one location in the span of about one month's time. The Israelites were camped in the central rift valley east of the Jordan River (see 1:1). In the book of Numbers, this location is referred to as "the plains of Moab," an area north of the Arnon River across the Jordan River from Jericho (see 36:13). It had been almost forty years since the Israelites had left Egypt.

The book of Deuteronomy concentrates on events that take place in the final weeks of Moses' life. The major event is the verbal communication of divine revelation from Moses to the Israelites (see 1:1–30:20; 31:30–32:47; 33:1–29). Other events include Moses' recording the law in a book and commissioning Joshua as the new leader (see 31:1–29), Moses' viewing of the land of Canaan from Mount Nebo (see 32:48–52; 34:1–4), and Moses' death (see 34:5–12).

The original recipients of Deuteronomy, both in its verbal and written presentations, were the second generation of the nation of Israel. All of that generation from forty to sixty years of age (except Joshua and Caleb, who were older) had been born in Egypt and had participated as children or teens in the Exodus. Those under forty had been born and reared in the wilderness. Together, they comprised the generation that was on the verge of conquering the land of Canaan under Joshua, forty years after they had left Egypt (see 1:34–39).

HISTORICAL AND THEOLOGICAL THEMES

Like Leviticus, the book of Deuteronomy contains much legal detail, but with an emphasis on the people rather than the priests. As Moses called the second generation of Israel to trust the Lord and be obedient to His covenant made at Sinai, he illustrated his points with references to Israel's past history. He reminded the Israelites of their rebellion against the Lord at Horeb (Sinai) and Kadesh (see 9:7–10:11; 1:26–46), which brought devastating consequences.

Most importantly, Moses called the people to take the land that God had promised by oath to their forefathers Abraham, Isaac, and Jacob (see 1:8; 6:10;

9:5; 29:13; 30:20; 34:4). Moses looked not only back but also ahead and saw that Israel's future failure to obey God would lead to her being scattered among the nations before the fulfillment of God's oath to the patriarchs would be completed (see 4:25–31; 29:22–30:10; 31:26–29).

The book of Deuteronomy, along with Psalms and Isaiah, reveals much about the attributes of God. Thus, it is directly quoted over forty times in the New Testament, exceeded only by Psalms and Isaiah, and has many more allusions to its content. Deuteronomy reveals that the Lord is the only God (see 4:39; 6:4) and that He is jealous, faithful, loving, merciful, and yet angered by sin (see 4:24; 7:9, 13; 4:31; 6:15 respectively). Moses repeats the phrase, "the LORD your God," to the people more than 250 times. He calls Israel to obey, fear, love, and serve God by walking in His ways and keeping His commandments (see 28:2; 10:12–13). By obeying Him, the people of Israel would receive His blessings (see 28:1–14). Obedience and the pursuit of personal holiness is based on the character of God. Because of who He is, His people are to be holy (see 7:6–11; 8:6, 11, 18; 10:12, 16, 17; 11:13; 13:3–4; 14:1–2).

INTERPRETIVE CHALLENGES

Three interpretive challenges face the reader of Deuteronomy. First, is the book a singular record, or is it only a part of the larger literary whole, the Pentateuch? The remainder of the Bible always views the Pentateuch as a unit, so the ultimate meaning of Deuteronomy cannot be divorced from its context in the Pentateuch. The book also assumes the reader is already familiar with the four books that precede it. In fact, Deuteronomy brings into focus all that had been revealed in Genesis to Numbers, as well as its implications for the people as they entered the land. However, every available Hebrew manuscript divides the Pentateuch in exactly the same way as the present text. This indicates that the book is a well-defined unit recounting the final speeches of Moses to Israel and that it may also be viewed as a singular record.

Second, is the structure of Deuteronomy based on the secular treaties of Moses' day? In recent decades, many evangelical scholars have supported the Mosaic authorship of Deuteronomy by appealing to the similarities between the structure of the book and the Ancient Near Eastern treaty form of the mid-second millennium BC (the approximate time of Moses). These secular *suzerainty* treaties (a ruler dictating his will to his vassals) followed a set pattern not used in the mid-first millennium BC. These treaties usually contained the following elements: (1) preamble, identifying the parties to the covenant; (2) historical prologue, a history of the king's dealing with his vassals; (3) general and specific stipulations; (4) witnesses; (5) blessings and curses; and (6) oaths and covenant ratification.

While there is agreement that Deuteronomy 1:1–5 is a preamble, 1:5–4:43 a historical prologue, and chapters 27–28 feature blessings and cursings, there is no consensus as to how the rest of the book fits the *suzerainty* structure. While there might have been a covenant renewal on the plains of Moab, this is neither clearly explicit nor implicit in Deuteronomy. Thus, it is best to take the book for what it claims to be: the explanation of the law given by Moses for the new generation. The structure follows the speeches given by Moses.

Third, what was the covenant made in the land of Moab, as referenced in Deuteronomy 29:1? The majority view is that this covenant is a renewal of the Sinaitic Covenant made nearly forty years before with the first generation. Moses simply updates and renews that same covenant with the second generation of Israel. A second view sees this covenant as a Palestinian Covenant, which guarantees the nation of Israel's right to the land, both at that time and in the future. A third position is that Moses in Deuteronomy 29–30 anticipated the New Covenant, since he knew Israel would fail to keep the Sinaitic Covenant. The third view seems the best.

LEGISLATION FOR THE LAITY

Leviticus 1:1–6:7

DRAWING NEAR

What is the first thing that comes to mind when you hear the word *sacrifice*?

_____

_____

_____

_____

_____

_____

_____

_____

THE CONTEXT

Everything had changed for the children of Israel. For 430 years, God's beloved people had lived in Egypt, away from the land that He had given to their forefather Abraham. They had served as slaves for many of those years. But now God had raised up a man named Moses to lead them back to their homeland. The people had witnessed God's power when He sent the ten plagues against Egypt (see Exodus 7–12), delivered them through the Red Sea (see Exodus 14), and given them water and manna in the wilderness (see Exodus 15–17).

God had led His people to the foot of Mount Sinai, where He would once again reveal His power by giving them His law and providing a foundation on which His people were to build their lives (see Exodus 19). The book of Leviticus contains those laws that God gave to the Israelites. The Lord has always intended His people to be holy—set apart—as He is holy, and from Israel's inception as a nation, He had called them to the same standard.

The people of God had offered sacrifices to Him since the time of Abel and Cain (see Genesis 4:3–4). But now, for the first time, the Lord gave a codified set of sacrifices by which they were worship Him. In this lesson, we will look at the first five chapters of Leviticus, which collectively establish the rules and regulations for five such sacrifices. The first three of these were voluntary; the last two, compulsory: (1) burnt offerings (see Leviticus 1:1–17), (2) grain offerings (see 2:1–16), (3) peace offerings (see 3:1–17), (4) sin offerings (see 4:1–5:13), and (5) trespass offerings (see 5:14–6:7).

All of these offerings were the means that God gave to His people for worshiping Him in righteousness, to give proper expression to penitent and thankful hearts. The rituals themselves didn't make the people righteous (see Hebrews 10:4). But for those who loved God and belonged to Him, they represented true expressions of their faith and worship.

KEYS TO THE TEXT

Read Leviticus 1:1–6:7, noting the key words and phrases indicated below.

REGULATIONS FOR BURNT OFFERINGS: God instructs Moses on how the people should perform the burnt offerings within the tabernacle.

1:1. NOW THE LORD CALLED TO MOSES: Leviticus begins where Exodus left off. No sooner did the glory cloud come down to rest on the tabernacle in the concluding verses of Exodus than God instructed Moses with the content in Leviticus. The question of how to use the tabernacle in worship is answered here by an audible voice from the divine glory over the ark in the Holy of Holies (see Exodus 40:34; Numbers 7:89; Psalm 80:1).

TABERNACLE OF MEETING: This was so named because it was the place where Israel would gather to meet the Lord (see Exodus 25:8, 22; 26:1–37). (Refer to the illustration on page 3.)

2. SPEAK TO THE CHILDREN OF ISRAEL: This is essential revelation, with reference to the people's spiritual life, for all the descendants of Jacob, who was also called Israel (see Genesis 32:28).

WHEN ANY ONE OF YOU BRINGS: These were completely voluntary and freewill offerings, with no specific number or frequency given (see Leviticus 1:3).

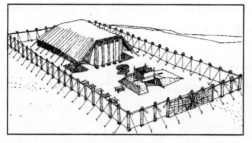

The tabernacle was to provide a place where God might dwell among His people. The term *tabernacle* sometimes refers to the tent, including the Holy Place and the Most Holy Place, which was covered with embroidered curtains. But in other places it refers to the entire complex, including the curtained court in which the tent stood.

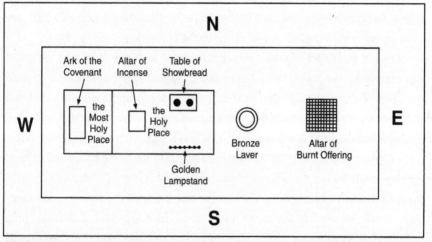

This illustration shows relative positions of the tabernacle furniture used in Israelite worship. The tabernacle is enlarged for clarity.

The regulation excluded horses, dogs, pigs, camels, and donkeys, which were used in pagan sacrifices, as well as rabbits, deer, beasts, and birds of prey. The sacrifice had to be from the offerers' herds, or they had to purchase it.

AN OFFERING: The Pharisees would later manipulate this simple concept so that adult children could selfishly withhold the material goods that would help their parents, under the guise of "Corban," that it was dedicated to the Lord (see Mark 7:8–13).

OF THE HERD AND OF THE FLOCK: These terms refer to the cattle (see Leviticus 1:3), sheep, or goats (see verse 10), respectively. Only domestic animals could be sacrificed.

3–17. IF HIS OFFERING: The burnt offerings were the first sacrifices revealed because these were the ones to be most frequently offered: every morning and evening (see Numbers 28:1–8), every Sabbath (see 28:9–10), the first day of each month (see 28:11–15), and at the special feasts (see 28:16–29:40). This offering signified voluntary and complete dedication and consecration to the Lord. It was an offering of repentance for sins committed, with the desire to be purged from the guilt of sinful acts. Designed to demonstrate the sinner's penitence and obedience, it indicated his self-dedication to the worship of God. The costliest animal was mentioned first, the least costly, last. The singing of psalms later became a part of this ritual (see Psalms 4; 5; 40; 50; 66).

BURNT SACRIFICE: This offering was so called because it required that the animal be completely consumed by the fire, except for the feathers of a bird (see 1:16) or the skin of the bull, which went to the priest (see verse 6; 7:8).

A MALE WITHOUT BLEMISH: Since no animal with any deformity or defect was permitted, the priests would inspect each animal, perhaps using a method which the Egyptians employed in their sacrifices, calling for all inspected and approved animals to have a certificate attached to the horns and sealed with wax. A male without blemish was required, as it was the choicest offering of the flock.

AT THE DOOR . . . BEFORE THE LORD: This entrance to the courtyard around the tabernacle where the altar of burnt offering stood (see Exodus 40:6) would place the person offering a sacrifice on the north side of the altar (see Leviticus 1:11). God's presence in the cloud rested upon the mercy seat of the ark in the Holy of Holies inside the tabernacle proper. The offering was offered before the Lord, not before man.

4. PUT HIS HAND ON THE HEAD: This symbolic gesture pictured the transfer of the sacrificer's sin to the sacrificial animal and was likely done with a prayer of repentance and request for forgiveness (see Psalm 51:18–19).

ON HIS BEHALF: This was a substitutionary sacrifice that prefigured the ultimate substitute—Jesus Christ (see Isaiah 53).

MAKE ATONEMENT: The word means "cover." The psalmist defines it by saying, "Blessed is he whose transgression is forgiven, whose sin is covered" (Psalm 32:1). Theologically, the "atonement" of the Old Testament covered sin only temporarily, but it did not eliminate sin or later judgment (see Hebrews 10:4). The one-time sacrifice of Jesus Christ fully atoned for sin, thus satisfying God's wrath forever and ensuring eternal salvation (see 9:12; 1 John 2:2), even to those who put saving faith in God for their redemption before Christ's death on the cross (see Romans 3:25–26; Hebrews 9:15).

5. HE SHALL KILL: Making vivid and dramatic the consequences of sin, the person offering the sacrifice killed and butchered the animal (see Leviticus 1:6).

AARON'S SONS: This refers to the immediate descendants of Aaron (Nadab, Abihu, Eleazar, and Ithamar; see Exodus 28:1). In the beginning, there were five priests, including Aaron, who served as the high priest.

SHALL BRING . . . SPRINKLE THE BLOOD: The priest had to collect the blood in a basin and then offer it to God as a sacrifice to indicate that a life had been taken; that is, a death had occurred (see Leviticus 17:11, 14). The price of sin is always death (see Genesis 2:17; Romans 6:23).

THE ALTAR: The altar of burnt offering (see Exodus 27:1–8; 38:1–7), which is in the courtyard outside of the tabernacle proper. (Refer to the illustration on page 3.) The prototype experience, before the tabernacle was constructed, is remembered in Exodus 24:1–8.

9. WASH ITS ENTRAILS: This allowed the person sacrificing to cleanse the animal of excrement and, thus, make it clean.

A SWEET AROMA: The pleasant smell of burning meat signified the sacrifice of obedience that was pleasing to the Lord. While the costly ritual recognized God's anger for sin committed (see Leviticus 1:13, 17), the penitent heart behind the sacrifice made it acceptable. That was far more significant than the sacrifice itself (see Genesis 8:21; 1 Samuel 15:22). This is the first of three freewill offerings to please the Lord. The others include the grain offering (see Leviticus 2:2) and the peace offering (see 3:5).

10–13. OF THE FLOCKS: This section in Leviticus describes the sacrifice of sheep and goats.

11. NORTH SIDE: This placed the person sacrificing in front of the tabernacle door (see 1:3).

14–17. OF BIRDS: This section describes the sacrifice of birds. God does not ask the poor to bring the same burnt offering as those financially well off because the relative cost to the one sacrificing was an important factor. This was the kind of sacrifice Joseph and Mary brought on the eighth day after Christ's birth for Mary's purification (see Luke 2:22–24).

15. THE PRIEST . . . WRING OFF ITS HEAD: Unlike the livestock being killed by the one offering the sacrifice, the bird was killed by the priest.

16. CROP . . . FEATHERS: This refers to the neck or gullet of a bird, where food was stored.

EAST SIDE . . . PLACE FOR ASHES: This was the closest side to the entrance of the tabernacle compound and provided for the easiest removal of the ashes outside (see Leviticus 6:10–11).

REGULATIONS FOR GRAIN OFFERINGS: God now instructs Moses on how the people should offer burnt offerings of grains, rather than animals.

2:1. A GRAIN OFFERING: This offering signified homage and thanksgiving to God as a voluntary offering that is offered along with a burnt offering and a drink offering at the appointed sacrifices (see Numbers 28:1–15). Three variations were prescribed: (1) uncooked flour (see Leviticus 2:1–3), (2) baked flour (see 2:4–13), or (3) roasted firstfruit grain from the harvest (see 2:14–16). This is the only non-animal sacrifice of the five and shows that there was a place for offering from the fruit of the soil (as in the case of Cain in Genesis 4). Refer to Leviticus 6:14–23 for the priests' instructions.

2. FINE FLOUR: The first variation consisted of uncooked flour whose "fine" quality paralleled the "unblemished" animal in the burnt offering. A portion of this offering was to support the priests (see 2:3). Like the drink offering or "libation," the grain offering was added to the burnt offering (see Numbers 28:1–15).

HANDFUL: Unlike the whole burnt offering (see Leviticus 1:9), only a representative or memorial portion was given to the Lord.

3. AARON'S AND HIS SONS': Unlike the burnt offering (see 1:9, 13, 17), this offering supplies provision for the priests.

MOST HOLY: This was unique from the others because it was not limited to God alone, like the burnt offering, nor eaten in part by the worshiper, like the peace offering. Only the priest could eat the portion not burned (see 7:9). The sin offering (see 6:17, 25) and the trespass offering (see 6:17; 7:1) are also called "most holy."

4–13. GRAIN OFFERING BAKED IN THE OVEN: This variation of the grain offering involved baked flour. The kinds of containers discussed include: (1) oven (see 2:4), (2) griddle (see verses 5–6), and (3) covered pan (see verses 7–10). The manner of preparation is discussed in verses 11–13.

UNLEAVENED CAKES: The notion of leaven as a symbol representing the presence of sin remains valid beyond the context of the Passover and continues to the New Testament (see Matthew 16:6; 1 Corinthians 5:6–7).

ANOINTED WITH OIL: Anointing is usually reserved for human appointments by God. Here, it was applied to the preparation of a holy sacrifice, set apart as a memorial to the Lord.

11. NO GRAIN OFFERING WHICH YOU BRING TO THE LORD: This applies to the offerings of Leviticus 2:4–10, all of which were to be burned on the altar.

NO LEAVEN NOR ANY HONEY: Both yeast and honey were edible foods but were never to be used with a grain offering, as both could induce fermentation, which symbolized sin.

12. AS FOR THE OFFERING OF THE FIRSTFRUITS: This applies to the offerings in verses 14–16, which were not to be burned on the altar but roasted by the worshiper (see verse 14) before going to the tabernacle.

13. THE SALT OF THE COVENANT: This was included in all of the offerings listed in verses 4–10, 14–16, since salt was emblematic of permanence or loyalty to the covenant.

14. FIRSTFRUITS: These would be offered at the Feast of Firstfruits (see 23:9–14) and the Feast of Weeks (see 23:15–22).

15. FRANKINCENSE: A gum resin with a pungent, balsamic odor, used for the incense in the tabernacle sacrifices (see Exodus 30:34).

REGULATIONS FOR PEACE OFFERINGS: God instructs Moses on how the people should make peace offerings, which were one of Israel's voluntary expressions of worship.

3:1–17. A PEACE OFFERING: The peace offering symbolized the peace and fellowship between the true worshiper and God (as a voluntary offering). It was the third freewill offering resulting in a sweet aroma to the Lord (see Leviticus 3:5), which served as the appropriate corollary to the burnt offering of atonement and the grain offering of consecration and dedication. It symbolized the fruit of redemptive reconciliation between a sinner and God (see 2 Corinthians 5:18). Refer to Leviticus 7:11–36 for the priests' instructions.

OF THE HERD: This pertains to cattle used in the peace offering.

MALE OR FEMALE: This is similar to the burnt offering in manner of presentation (see 1:3–9), but different in that a female was allowed.

4. THE FAT: All of the fat was dedicated to the Lord (see 3:3–5, 9–11, 14–16).

6–11. OF THE FLOCK: This pertains to sheep used in the peace offering.

11. AS FOOD: The sacrifice was intended to symbolize a meal between God and the one offering it, where peace and friendship were epitomized by sharing that meal together.

12–16. A GOAT: This pertains to goats used in the peace offering.

17. NEITHER FAT NOR BLOOD: The details given in the chapter distinctly define which fat was to be burned and not eaten, so that whatever adhered to other parts or was mixed with them might be eaten. As with many facets of the Mosaic legislation, there were underlying health benefits also.

REGULATIONS FOR SIN OFFERINGS: God instructs Moses on how the people should give offerings intended to make atonement for their unknown or unintentional sins.

4:1. NOW THE LORD SPOKE TO MOSES: The sin offerings (see 4:1–5:13) and trespass offerings (see 5:14–6:7) differ from the previous three in that the former were voluntary and these were compulsory. The sin offering differs from the trespass offering in that the former involved iniquity where restitution was not possible, while in the latter it was possible. The sin offering also atoned for sins committed unknowingly—unintentional sins of commission (see 4:1–35) and omission (see 5:1–13). Leviticus 4:1–35 deals with the person committing the sin: (1) the high priest (verses 3–12), (2) the congregation (verses 13–21), (3) a leader (verses 22–26), or (4) an individual (verses 27–35). Leviticus 5:1–13 unfolds according to the animal sacrificed: (1) lamb/goat (verses 1–6), (2) bird (verses 7–10), and then (3) flour (verses 11–13). Refer to 6:24–30 for the priests' instructions.

2. SINS UNINTENTIONALLY: The intended meaning is to stray into a sinful situation, but not necessarily to be taken completely by surprise. Numbers 15:30–31 illustrates the defiant attitude of intentional sin.

OUGHT NOT . . . DOES ANY: Sins of commission.

3. IF THE ANOINTED PRIEST SINS: This section (through verse 12) describes the sacrifices for the sin of the anointed priest. See Exodus 29:29 and Leviticus 16:32, which define this person as the high priest.

BRINGING GUILT ON THE PEOPLE: Only the high priest, due to his representative position, was capable of this type of infusion of guilt. For example, although Achan brought about the defeat of all Israel when he held back the banned spoils, the entire nation was not executed, as he and his family were (see Joshua 7:22–26).

5. TO THE TABERNACLE: He actually went into the Holy Place.

6. SEVEN TIMES: The number of completion or perfection, indicating the nature of God's forgiveness (see Psalm 103:12).

THE VEIL OF THE SANCTUARY: The veil marked the entry into the very presence of God in the Holy of Holies.

7. ALTAR OF SWEET INCENSE: See Exodus 30:1–10. This altar was in the tabernacle proper, before the veil. It was so close to the ark that Hebrews speaks of it as actually being in the Holy of Holies (see Hebrews 9:4). This altar was also sprinkled with blood on the Day of Atonement (see Exodus 30:10).

ALTAR . . . BURNT OFFERING: The altar in the courtyard on which blood was normally splashed.

11. OFFAL: This term identifies the major internal organs of an animal, including the intestines' waste content.

12. CARRY OUTSIDE THE CAMP: This was a symbolic gesture of removing the sin from the people (see Hebrews 13:11–13 in reference to Christ).

13–21. THE WHOLE CONGREGATION: Sacrifices for the sin of the congregation were to follow essentially the same procedure as that for the sin of priests (see Leviticus 4:3–12).

22–26. A RULER HAS SINNED: These are sacrifices for the sin of a ruler. The blood of the sacrifice was not sprinkled in the Holy Place, as for the priest or congregation (see verses 6, 17), but only on the altar of burnt offering.

27–35. THE COMMON PEOPLE: These are sacrifices for the sin of an individual. Either a goat (see verses 27–31) or a lamb (see verses 32–35) could be sacrificed in much the same manner as the offering for a ruler (see verses 22–26).

5:1. IF A PERSON SINS: Dealing with unintentional sins continues in this section with an emphasis on sins of omission (see 5:1–4). The call to confession named a few examples of violations for which penitence was the right response: (1) withholding evidence (see verse 1), (2) touching something unclean (see verses 2–3), and (3) rash oath-making (see verse 4). Lambs/goats (see verse 6), birds (see verses 7–10), or flour (see verses 11–13) were acceptable sacrifices.

OATH . . . WITNESS: A witness who did not come forward to testify was sinning when he had actually seen a violation or had firsthand knowledge, such as hearing the violator confess to the sin.

4. SWEARS: "Speaking thoughtlessly" suggests a reckless oath for good or bad—that is, an oath the speaker should not or could not keep.

5. HE SHALL CONFESS: Confession must accompany the sacrifice as the outward expression of a repentant heart which openly acknowledged agreement with God concerning sin. Sacrifice without true faith, repentance, and obedience was hypocrisy (see Psalm 26:4; Isaiah 9:17; Amos 5:21–26).

9

11. EPHAH: About six gallons.

NO OIL . . . FRANKINCENSE: Contrast the grain offering (see Leviticus 2:2).

REGULATIONS FOR TRESPASS OFFERINGS: The trespass offering symbolized an atonement for sin unknowingly committed, where restitution was possible.

5:15. IF A PERSON COMMITS A TRESPASS: Like the sin offering (see Leviticus 4:1–5:13), this one was compulsory. For sins against the Lord's property, restitution was made to the priest (see 5:14–19), while restitution was made to the person who suffered loss in other instances (see 6:1–7).

SHEKEL OF THE SANCTUARY: This amounted to twenty gerahs (see Exodus 30:13; Leviticus 27:25; Numbers 3:47) or two bekahs (see Exodus 38:26), which is the equivalent of four-tenths of one ounce. God fixed the value of a shekel.

16. ONE-FIFTH: The offender was required to make a 120 percent restitution, which was considerably lower than that prescribed elsewhere in the Mosaic law (see, for example, Exodus 22:7, 9). Perhaps this is accounted for by a voluntary confession in contrast to an adjudicated and forced conviction.

6:1–7. While all sins are against God (see Psalm 51:4), some are direct (see Leviticus 5:14–19) while others are indirect, involving people, as given in this section. These violations are not exhaustive but representative samples used to establish and illustrate the principle.

6. YOUR VALUATION: The priest served as an appraiser to give appropriate value to the goods in question.

UNLEASHING THE TEXT

1) How was sacrifice an act of worship to the Lord?

_____

_____

_____

_____

_____

_____

_____

_____

_____

2) Which of the five sacrifices described in Leviticus 1–5 were voluntary? What does this tell us about the nature of each sacrifice?

_____

_____

_____

_____

_____

_____

3) What rituals or practices were present in several of the sacrifices?

_____

_____

_____

_____

_____

4) What are some of the key images that repeat throughout these chapters? What do those images represent?

_____

_____

_____

_____

_____

EXPLORING THE MEANING

Sacrifice revealed the seriousness of sin. When modern readers of the Bible encounter the idea of sacrifice in the Old Testament, it is easy to process that concept in a purely academic sense—meaning, we have knowledge of what happened during these rituals: Families would gather at the tabernacle (and later at the temple) to offer a sacrifice either as a voluntary expression of worship or as a means of receiving forgiveness for sins. Yet the actual experience of offering a sacrifice would have been much more real and memorable.

Leviticus 1 gives us an overview of the process: "If his offering is a burnt sacrifice of the herd, let him offer a male without blemish; he shall offer it of his own free will at the door of the tabernacle of meeting before the LORD. Then he shall put his hand on the head of the burnt offering, and it will be accepted on his behalf to make atonement for him. He shall kill the bull before the LORD; and the priests, Aaron's sons, shall bring the blood and sprinkle the blood all around on the altar that is by the door of the tabernacle of meeting" (verses 3–5).

Imagine being a child and witnessing such a sacrifice. You see your father lead a lamb or bull to the entrance of the tabernacle. It is alive. It snorts and pulls against the rope that binds it. After a conversation with the priests, your father places his hand on the animal's head. You realize something significant is happening. With a quick motion, your father unsheathes a knife and cuts the animal's throat. You don't just see the blood, you smell it. You hear the sound it makes pooling on the ground. You watch as the priests begin dragging the now-lifeless carcass into the tabernacle compound, where it will be butchered and its pieces burned.

The message would be crystal clear. Sin is serious. Sin leads to death, because God is utterly righteous and perfectly just. And sin can only be covered over with blood.

Sacrifice revealed the importance of atonement. In addition to highlighting the seriousness of sin, the sacrificial system established in Leviticus also revealed the necessity of atonement as the only method for dealing with sin. Look again at Moses' instructions in Leviticus 1: "Then he shall put his hand on the head of the burnt offering, and it will be accepted on his behalf to make atonement for him" (verse 4).

The phrase "make atonement" is repeated often throughout Leviticus. The Hebrew word for "atonement" means "to cover." Specifically, God revealed through His instructions to Moses that sin can only be forgiven—and the penalty of sin fulfilled—when it is covered over with blood. As the author of Hebrews wrote, "According to the law almost all things are purified with blood, and without shedding of blood there is no remission" (9:22).

Importantly, the sacrifices required in the Old Testament law produced only a temporary atonement. The blood of bulls and goats represented God's plan for establishing purity within the Israelite community through regular and continual sacrifices. However, His plan always included the more perfect sacrifice offered by Jesus Christ, which produced a permanent atonement for sin.

The author of Hebrews states it this way: "Not with the blood of goats and calves, but with His own blood He entered the Most Holy Place once for all, having obtained eternal redemption. For if the blood of bulls and goats and the ashes of a heifer, sprinkling the unclean, sanctifies for the purifying of the flesh, how much more shall the blood of Christ, who through the eternal Spirit offered Himself without spot to God, cleanse your conscience from dead works to serve the living God?" (9:12–14).

Sacrifice was a means of provision for the priests. One element of the sacrificial system that is often underappreciated is the way God used that system to provide for the priests and Levites within the community. When a sacrifice was made, only a portion was physically burned on the altar. If the offering was an animal, much of the meat was returned to the family who provided the offering, and it was eaten by that family as a time of celebration and worship before God. However, some of the meat was also provided to the priests.

We find a good example of this practice in Leviticus 2 in the description of the grain offering, which was a voluntary offering of grain or other produce. "He shall bring it to Aaron's sons, the priests, one of whom shall take from it his handful of fine flour and oil with all the frankincense. And the priest shall burn it as a memorial on the altar, an offering made by fire, a sweet aroma to the LORD. The rest of the grain offering shall be Aaron's and his sons'. It is most holy of the offerings to the LORD made by fire" (verses 2–3).

This practice was of critical importance within the Israelite community, especially after they took possession of the promised land. Every other tribe in Israel was given specific regions of that land to make their own—to farm, to build houses, to establish business, and so on. However, the Levites received no land. Instead, they concentrated on serving God and carrying out the practical elements of the sacrificial system. In return, their needs were provided for by receiving portions of those sacrifices.

REFLECTING ON THE TEXT

5) When have you been confronted by the seriousness of sin?

_____

_____

_____

_____

_____

_____

_____

6) How do you respond to the reality that only blood can atone for sin?

_____

_____

_____

_____

7) What are some ways the sacrifices described in Leviticus 1–5 point forward to the perfect sacrifice of Jesus on the cross?

_____

_____

_____

_____

8) How are pastors and other ministers provided for within the church today?

_____

_____

_____

_____

PERSONAL RESPONSE

9) What are some practical ways you can remind yourself of the seriousness of sin this week?

_____

_____

_____

_____

10) Are there any areas of sin in your life that you have not dealt with? What steps can you take to remedy that?

_____

_____

_____

_____

2

LEGISLATION FOR THE PRIESTHOOD
Leviticus 6:8–10:20

DRAWING NEAR
Why do you think God was so particular that His priests follow His instructions exactly?

_____

_____

_____

_____

_____

THE CONTEXT
The sacrificial system provided the foundation for the Israelites' new national identity and community as God's free people. It was God's gracious revelation by which His people could live in holy, right relationship to Him. It also gave Israel the means to express their worship and devotion to God before the watchful surrounding nations. The law clearly defined their duties for worship and the sacrifices in the tabernacle and for the individual worshiper and the nation's covenantal relationship to God.

In the previous lesson, we examined the five major sacrifices included in that system: (1) the burnt offering, (2) the grain offering, (3) the peace offering, (4) the sin offering, and (5) the trespass offering (see Leviticus 1:1–6:7). This time, we will take a closer look at God's regulations regarding these offerings. We will then observe how the offerings were actually performed for the first time by Moses, Aaron, and the first generation of priests, as, unfortunately, the initiation of the sacrificial system did not unfold as planned.

Leviticus 10 recounts the deaths of two of Aaron's sons the first time they ministered as priests before God because they did not follow God's regulations. That event would have shocked the community, highlighting once again the reality that the wages of sin is death and that God's holiness has practical consequences for His people.

KEYS TO THE TEXT

Read Leviticus 6:8–10:20, noting the key words and phrases indicated below.

> INSTRUCTIONS FOR THE PRIESTS: *The opening chapters of Leviticus explore five major offerings from the worshiper's perspective. Now, instructions for the priests are given, with special attention given to the priests' portion of the sacrifice.*

6:8–13. This section returns to address the burnt offering (see Leviticus 1:3–17).

9. ON THE HEARTH UPON THE ALTAR ALL NIGHT: This resulted in the complete incineration of the sacrifice, picturing it as totally given to the Lord, with the smoke arising as a sweet aroma to Him (see 1:9, 13, 17).

10. TAKE UP THE ASHES OF THE BURNT OFFERING: This described both the immediate (see 6:10) and final (see verse 11) disposition of the ash remains (that which is worthless).

13. ALWAYS BE BURNING: The perpetual flame indicated a continuous readiness on the part of God to receive confession and restitution through the sacrifice.

14–23. The grain offering (see 2:1–16).

16–18. THE REMAINDER OF IT AARON AND HIS SONS SHALL EAT: Unlike the burnt offering, the grain offering provided food for the priests and their male children (that is, future priests).

16. IN A HOLY PLACE: This was to be eaten only in the courtyard of the tabernacle.

19–23. THE OFFERING OF AARON AND HIS SONS: Aaron, as high priest, was to make a daily grain offering at morning and night on behalf of his priestly family.

22. THE PRIEST FROM AMONG HIS SONS, WHO IS ANOINTED IN HIS PLACE: The high priests who succeed Aaron are in view here.

IT SHALL BE WHOLLY BURNED: The priests' offering was to be given completely, with nothing left over.

26. PRIEST WHO OFFERS IT FOR SIN SHALL EAT IT: The priest putting the offering on the brazen altar could use it for food, if the sacrifice was for a ruler (see 4:22–26) or the people (see 4:27–35).

27–28. These are instructions on the cleanliness of the priest's garments as they relate to blood.

30. NO SIN OFFERING . . . EATEN: Those sacrifices made on behalf of a priest (see 4:3–12) or the congregation (see 4:13–21) could not be eaten.

7.1: THIS IS THE LAW OF THE TRESPASS OFFERING: Verses 1–10 return to the trespass offering (see 5:14–6:7). Verses 7–10 provide a brief excursus on what may be eaten by the priests.

10. MIXED WITH OIL OR DRY: Both were acceptable options.

11–36. THIS IS THE LAW OF THE SACRIFICE OF PEACE OFFERINGS: This section returns to the peace offering (see 3:1–17). The purposes for the peace offering are given in verses 11–18. Special instructions which prevented a priest from being "cut off" (see verses 19–27) and the allotment to Aaron and his sons (see verses 28–36) are enumerated.

11–15. A peace offering for thanksgiving was also to be combined with a grain offering (see 2:1–16). The meat had to be eaten that same day, probably for the reason of health (as it would rapidly spoil) and for the purpose of preventing people from thinking that such meat had some spiritual presence in it, thus developing some superstitions.

13. HE SHALL OFFER LEAVENED BREAD WITH THE SACRIFICE: Contrast the unleavened grain offering (see 2:11).

16–18. IF THE SACRIFICE OF HIS OFFERING IS A VOW OR . . . VOLUNTARY: The priest could eat the meat the same day or the next day, but eating on the third day brought punishment.

19–21. THAT PERSON SHALL BE CUT OFF: Uncleanness was punishable by death. (See Leviticus 22 for more details.)

22–27. See note on 3:17.

29–33. BRING HIS OFFERING TO THE LORD FROM THE SACRIFICE OF HIS PEACE OFFERING: The worshiper made a peace offering from his sacrifice so that the Lord received the blood and the fat (see 7:33). The priests received the breast (see verses 30–31) and right thigh (see verse 33). The worshiper could use the rest for himself.

30–34. WAVE OFFERING . . . HEAVE OFFERING: These were symbolic acts indicating the offering was for the Lord. Bread (see Exodus 29:23–24), meat (see 29:22–24), gold (see 38:24), oil (see Leviticus 14:12), and grain (see 23:11) all served as wave offerings. Heave offerings are far less numerous (see Exodus 29:27–28; Deuteronomy 12:6, 11, 17). Jewish tradition portrayed the wave offering as being presented with a horizontal motion and the heave offering with a vertical motion, as suggested by Leviticus 10:15. Leviticus 9:21 refers to both as a wave offering.

37–38. THIS IS THE LAW: Moses gives a summary conclusion of 1:3–7:36.

37. THE CONSECRATIONS: This refers to the offerings at the ordination of Aaron and his sons (see 8:14–36; Exodus 29:1–46).

INSTITUTING THE AARONIC PRIESTHOOD: *Before Aaron's time, the patriarchs and fathers had offered sacrifices to God, but only with Aaron came the fully prescribed priestly service.*

8:1–10:20. TAKE AARON AND HIS SONS: Aaron and his descendants (as well as the tribe of Levi) were selected by God to be Israel's priests—they did not appoint themselves to the position. Aaron and his sons were consecrated before they ministered to the Lord, described here with all the ceremonial details as it was done after the tabernacle was completed and the regulations for the various sacrifices enacted.

2. THE GARMENTS: The garments were designed to exalt the office and function of the priesthood, marking out Aaron as a special person playing a special mediatorial role—they were "holy" vestments. In the Old Testament priestly system for the nation of Israel, such dress maintained the priest-laity distinction.

THE ANOINTING OIL: Used for ceremonial anointing (see verses 12, 30).

7. THE EPHOD: Whenever Aaron entered the sanctuary, he carried with him on his shoulders the badge and the engraved stones that were representative of the twelve tribes of Israel (see Exodus 28:5–12).

8. HE PUT THE BREASTPLATE ON HIM: The twelve precious stones, each also engraved with one tribe's name, colorfully and ornately displayed Aaron's representative role of intercession for the tribes before the Lord. The breastplate was to be securely fastened to the ephod so as not to come loose from it (see Exodus

28:28; 39:21). Thus, to speak of the ephod after this was done would be to speak of the whole ensemble.

THE URIM AND THE THUMMIM: The etymological source of these two terms, as well as the material nature of the objects represented by them, cannot be established with any degree of finality. Clearly, two separate objects were inserted into the breastplate and became, thereby, an essential part of the high priest's official regalia. The passages in which the terms appear, and those which record inquiries of the Lord when a high priest with the ephod was present, allow for two conclusions: First, these two objects represented the right of the high priest to request guidance for the acknowledged leader who could not approach God directly, as had Moses, but had to come via the God-ordained priestly structure. Second, the revelation then received gave specific direction for an immediate problem and went beyond what could be associated with some sort of sacred lots providing merely a wordless "yes" and "no" response.

12. TO CONSECRATE HIM: This act ceremonially set Aaron apart from the congregation to be a priest unto God, and from the other priests to be high priest.

23–24. RIGHT EAR ... RIGHT HAND ... RIGHT FOOT: Using a part to represent the whole, Aaron and his sons were consecrated to listen to God's holy Word, to carry out His holy assignments, and to live holy lives.

35. KEEP THE CHARGE OF THE LORD: The commandment of God ordered Aaron and his sons to do exactly as the Lord had spoken through Moses. Disobedience would meet with death.

9:1. MOSES CALLED AARON AND HIS SONS: This section (through verse 24) describes the beginning of the priestly ministry. Since the priests had been consecrated and appropriate sacrifices offered on their behalf, they were prepared to fulfill their priestly duties on behalf of the congregation as they carried out all the prescribed sacrifices described in Leviticus 1–7 and rendered them to the Lord.

4, 6. THE GLORY OF THE LORD WILL APPEAR TO YOU: The Lord's manifestation or presence was going to appear to them to show acceptance of the sacrifices. (See notes on verses 23–24, where that appearance is recorded.)

8. AARON THEREFORE WENT TO THE ALTAR: Aaron now presents sacrifices on his own behalf (see verses 8–14) and on behalf of the people (see verses 15–21).

17. THE BURNT SACRIFICE OF THE MORNING: The Lord had provided these instructions: "The other lamb you shall offer at twilight; and you shall offer with

it the grain offering and the drink offering, as in the morning, for a sweet aroma, an offering made by fire to the LORD" (Exodus 29:41; see also Numbers 28:4).

22. LIFTED HIS HAND TOWARD THE PEOPLE: The high priest gave a symbolic gesture for blessing, perhaps pronouncing the priestly blessing (see Numbers 6:24–26; 2 Corinthians 13:14).

23. THE GLORY OF THE LORD APPEARED: The Bible speaks often of the glory of God—the visible appearance of His beauty and perfection in blazing light. His glory appeared to Moses in a burning bush in Midian (see Exodus 3:1–6), in a cloud on Mount Sinai (see 24:15–17), and in a rock on Mount Sinai (see 33:18–23). The glory of God also filled the tabernacle (see 40:34), led the people as a pillar of fire and cloud (see 40:35–38), and filled the temple in Jerusalem (see 1 Kings 8:10–11). Here, Leviticus records that when Aaron made the first sacrifice in the wilderness as a priest, the "glory of the LORD appeared to all the people." In these manifestations, God was revealing His righteousness, holiness, truth, wisdom, and grace—the sum of all He is. However, nowhere has God's glory been more perfectly expressed than in His Son, the Lord Jesus Christ (see John 1:14). It will be seen on earth again when He returns (see Matthew 24:29–31; 25:31).

24. FIRE CAME OUT . . . AND CONSUMED THE BURNT OFFERING: This fire miraculously signified that God had accepted their offering (see 1 Kings 18:38–39), and the people shouted for joy because of that acceptance and worshiped God.

> HOLY FIRE VS. PROFANE FIRE: *This section of Leviticus relates the tragic consequences that occurred when Nadab and Abihu, two sons of Aaron, violated God's prescriptions for offering incense.*

10:1. NADAB AND ABIHU: Aaron's two oldest sons. (Refer to the chart, "Priests in the Old Testament," on page 21.)

CENSER: The vessel in which the incense was burned in the Holy Place (its features are unknown) was to be used only for holy purposes.

PROFANE FIRE: Although the exact infraction is not detailed, in some way Nadab and Abihu violated the prescription for offering incense (see Exodus 30:9, 34–38), probably because they were drunk (see Leviticus 10:8–9). Instead of taking the incense fire from the brazen altar, they had some other source for the fire. Thus they perpetrated an act, which, considering the descent of the miraculous fire they had just seen and their solemn duty to do as God told them, betrayed

Priests in the Old Testament

Name	Identification	Scripture
Aaron	Older brother of Moses; first high priest of Israel	Exod. 28; 29
Nadab and Abihu	Evil sons of Aaron	Lev. 10:1–2
Eleazar and Ithamar	Godly sons of Aaron; Eleazar was Israel's second high priest	Lev. 10:6; Num. 20:26
Phineas	Son of Eleazar; Israel's third high priest whose zeal for pure worship stopped a plague	Num. 25:7–13
Eli	Descendant of Ithamar; raised Samuel at Shiloh	1 Sam. 1–4
Hophni and Phinehas	Evil sons of Eli	1 Sam. 2:12–36; 1 Sam. 4:17
Ahimelech	Led a priestly community at Nob; killed by Saul for befriending David	1 Sam. 21; 22
Abiathar	Son of Ahimelech who escaped the slaying at Nob	1 Sam. 22:20–23; 2 Sam. 20:25
Zadok	High priest during the reign of David and Solomon	2 Sam. 15; 20:25 1 Kings 1
Jehoiada	High priest who saved Joash from Queen Athaliah's purge	2 Kings 11; 12
Uriah	Priest who built pagan altar for evil King Ahaz	2 Kings 16:10-16
Hilkiah	High priest during the reign of Josiah	2 Kings 22; 23
Elishama and Jehoram	Teaching priests during the reign of Jehoshaphat	2 Chr. 17:7-9
Amariah	High priest of Bethel; confronted Amos the prophet	2 Chr. 19:11
Jahaziel	Levite who assured Jehoshaphat of deliverance from an enemy	2 Chr. 20:14-17
Azariah	High priest who stood against Uzziah when the ruler began to act as a prophet	2 Chr. 20:16-20
Ezra	Scribe, teacher, and priest during the rebuilding of Jerusalem after the Babylonian captivity	Ezra 7-10; Neh. 8
Eliashib	High priest during the time of Nehemiah	Neh. 3:1; 13:4- 5
Shelemiah	Priest during the time of Nehemiah; was in charge of administering storehouses	Neh. 13:13
Pashhur	False priest who persecuted the prophet Jeremiah	Jer. 20:1-6
Amaziah	Evil priest of Bethel; confronted Amos the prophet	Amos 7:10-17
Joshua	First high priest after the Babylonian captivity	Hag. 1 :1, 12; Zech. 3

carelessness, irreverence, and lack of consideration for God. Such a tendency had to be punished for all priests to see as a warning.

2. FIRE WENT OUT: The same divine fire that accepted the sacrifices (see 9:24) consumed the errant priests. This was not unlike the later deaths of Uzzah (see 2 Samuel 6:6–7) or Ananias and Sapphira (see Acts 5:5, 10).

3. I MUST BE REGARDED AS HOLY . . . I MUST BE GLORIFIED: Nadab and Abihu were guilty of violating both requirements of God's absolute standard. The priests had received repeated and solemn warnings regarding the necessity of reverence before God (see Exodus 19:22; 29:44).

AARON HELD HIS PEACE: Aaron, in spite of losing his two sons, did not complain but submitted to the righteous judgment of God.

4. MISHAEL . . . ELZAPHAN: Their father was Uzziel, the uncle of Aaron, Miriam, and Moses (see Exodus 6:18–22).

CARRY YOUR BRETHREN: This procedure prevented the priests from defiling themselves by handling the dead bodies (see Leviticus 21:1) and allowed the whole congregation to see the result of such disregard for the holiness of God.

OUT OF THE CAMP: As this was done with the ashes of sacrificed animals (see 6:11), so it was done with the remains of these two priests who received God's wrath.

6. ELEAZAR AND ITHAMAR: These are Aaron's youngest sons, who still lived. Later, the line of Eleazar would be designated as the unique line of the high priest (see Numbers 25:10–13).

DO NOT UNCOVER YOUR HEADS NOR TEAR YOUR CLOTHES: This prohibition against the customary signs of mourning was usually reserved for the high priest only, as prescribed in Leviticus 21:10–12. Here, Moses applies it to Eleazar and Ithamar also.

9. DO NOT DRINK WINE OR INTOXICATING DRINK: Taken in its context, this prohibition suggests that intoxication led Nadab and Abihu to perform their blasphemous act (see Proverbs 23:20–35; 1 Timothy 3:3; Titus 1:7).

11. THAT YOU MAY TEACH THE CHILDREN OF ISRAEL: It was essential that alcohol not hinder the clarity of the priests' minds, since they were to teach God's law to all of Israel. They were the expositors of the Scripture, alongside the prophets who received the Word directly from the Lord. Ezra would become the supreme example of a commendable priest (see Ezra 7:10).

16–18. MOSES MADE CAREFUL INQUIRY: The sin offering had not been eaten as prescribed in Leviticus 6:26 but, rather, it was wholly burned. It was the duty of the priests to have eaten the meat after the blood was sprinkled on the altar, but instead of eating it in a sacred feast, they had burned it outside the camp. Moses discovered this disobedience, probably from a dread of some further judgment, and challenged not Aaron, whose heart was too torn in the death of his sons, but the two surviving sons in the priesthood to explain their breach of ritual duty.

19. AARON SAID TO MOSES: Aaron, who heard the charge, and by whose direction the violation had occurred, gave the explanation. His reason was that his sons had done all the ritual sacrifice correctly up to the point of eating the meat but omitted eating because he was too dejected for a feast in the face of the appalling judgments that had fallen. He was wrong, because God had specifically commanded the sin offering to be eaten in the Holy Place. God's law was clear, and it was sin to deviate from it.

20. WHEN MOSES HEARD THAT, HE WAS CONTENT: Moses sympathized with Aaron's grief, and having made his point, dropped the issue.

UNLEASHING THE TEXT

1) What did God tell the priests to do concerning their garments after performing the burnt offering and sin offering? Why do you think He issued this command?

_____

_____

_____

2) Which of the offerings were the priests allowed to eat? What were they prohibited from eating? Why do you think God made this provision for them?

_____

_____

_____

3) What instructions did God give to Moses concerning Aaron and his sons?

_____

_____

_____

4) Why did Nadab and Abihu die? How could that tragedy have been prevented?

_____

_____

_____

EXPLORING THE MEANING

Fire was a symbol of God's presence. As we saw in the previous lesson, the burnt offering was one of five regular sacrifices performed by the priests at the tabernacle. However, the burnt offering was special in that it was performed every morning and every evening within the community—with no exceptions.

Because of the regularity of these sacrifices, God mandated on several occasions that the fire used to perform these offerings should never be extinguished. As He said to Moses, "Command Aaron and his sons, saying, 'This is the law of the burnt offering: The burnt offering shall be on the hearth upon the altar all night until morning, and the fire of the altar shall be kept burning on it'" (Leviticus 6:9). "A fire shall always be burning on the altar; it shall never go out" (verse 13).

Throughout Scripture, we see examples of God choosing to use fire as a way to represent His presence. (Think of Moses and the burning bush or of the pillar of fire that went before the Israelites during the Exodus from Egypt.) Therefore, God's instruction to keep the fire continually burning on the altar at His tabernacle was a visual representation of His continual presence in the community. Just as the fire was always burning, God was always present and ready to make atonement for the sins of His people that they might live in right fellowship with Him.

Anointing was a symbol of the Holy Spirit's presence. Leviticus 8 describes a critical moment for the new nation of Israel: the consecration of its priests. In obedience to God's command, Moses gathered the entire congregation of Israel at the entrance to the tabernacle to serve as witnesses for this important moment. Moses then went through a series of rituals to physically and spiritually cleanse Aaron and his sons and to set them apart as priests, sanctified for this particular service to God.

The act of anointing was a key element in this consecration. Specifically, Moses anointed the articles within the tabernacle along with the men who would serve as priests (see verses 10–12) with both oil and blood (see Hebrews 9:21): "Then Moses took some of the anointing oil and some of the blood which was on the altar, and sprinkled it on Aaron, on his garments, on his sons, and on the garments of his sons with him; and he consecrated Aaron, his garments, his sons, and the garments of his sons with him" (Leviticus 8:30).

As we have seen, the blood was required to make atonement for sin and to purify both article and priest—to make them holy. And what of the oil? Throughout Scripture, God used oil to symbolize the pouring out of His Holy Spirit. For instance, when David was anointed as the next king of Israel, we read that "Samuel took the horn of oil and anointed him in the midst of his brothers; and the Spirit of the LORD came upon David from that day forward" (1 Samuel

16:13). Just as Moses poured out the oil to anoint Aaron and his sons, so God poured out His Spirit to consecrate them as priests.

God's standard of holiness is perfect. Leviticus 10 begins with a shocking moment: "Then Nadab and Abihu, the sons of Aaron, each took his censer and put fire in it, put incense on it, and offered profane fire before the LORD, which He had not commanded them. So fire went out from the LORD and devoured them, and they died before the LORD" (verses 1–2).

It is not immediately clear to the modern reader what these men did wrong. The "profane fire" may have been a sacrifice that was not included in God's specific instructions. Or the priests may have been drunk while performing their service at the altar (see verses 8–10). What is clear is that Nadab and Abihu violated God's standard of holiness. They had witnessed a miracle just moments before, in which God sent divine fire to consume their offerings (see 9:24). Yet they immediately dishonored God by bringing sin into His very presence—so that same divine fire ended their lives.

The deaths of Nadab and Abihu were similar to the fate of a man we read about later in the Bible, named Uzzah. King David wanted to bring the Ark of the Covenant into Jerusalem, so he had the ark placed on a cart and wheeled into the city—against God's clear prescriptions for the ark's transportation (Numbers 3:30–31; 4:15; Exodus 25:12–15). When the oxen driving the cart stumbled, Uzzah put his hand out and touched the ark to stabilize it. As a result, he was struck dead instantly (see 2 Samuel 6:6–8).

In both instances, people paid with their lives because they did not fear God as they ought or treat Him with the reverence He deserves and demands. How wonderful that we who belong to Christ in faith have received His perfect righteousness (Philippians 3:9), which is why we are able to come into God's presence without fear. That is an amazing gift of God's grace alone!

REFLECTING ON THE TEXT

5) How did the sacrificial system emphasize the holiness of God and the high cost of Israel's sin?

_____

_____

_____

_____

6) How does the presence of the Holy Spirit inform the way you think about your sin?

_____

_____

_____

_____

7) How does God's holiness relate to your worship of Him? In what sense might your worship be "profane"?

_____

_____

_____

_____

8) Were Nadab and Abihu's deaths "fair"? Explain.

_____

_____

_____

_____

PERSONAL RESPONSE

9) How can you explain the concept of God's holiness in a way that makes sense to others?

_____

_____

_____

_____

10) What specific steps can you take to spend time enjoying God's presence this week?

_____

_____

_____

_____

3

PRESCRIPTIONS FOR UNCLEANNESS
Leviticus 11:1–16:34

DRAWING NEAR
Growing up, what were some "house rules" that you found especially difficult to follow? Why?

_____

_____

_____

_____

_____

THE CONTEXT
We have seen in previous lessons that holiness is a primary theme in the book of Leviticus. The first five chapters offered detailed instructions for specific sacrifices the Israelite community needed to make in order to atone for their sin. The next five chapters included further regulations for how the priests should carry out those sacrifices on behalf of all—as well as a tragic, vivid example of the penalty for violating God's holiness.

In this lesson, we will examine how the need to maintain holiness—a separation unto the Lord and from surrounding nations—impacted the everyday lives of God's people. Leviticus 11 focuses specifically on food. God designated certain animals clean and to be eaten of freely, while other animals made an Israelite unclean if eaten—and, in some cases, even if touched.

The remainder of the chapters in Leviticus covered in this lesson focus on regulations for maintaining ritual cleanliness in specific situations: childbirth, dealing with diseases and skin issues, and so on. In each of these cases, the physical ailment or infirmity did not equate to a blight on the person's character. Rather, the regulations God provided were a pathway for God's people to maintain holiness within the community so that God could continue to dwell in their midst without destroying them.

KEYS TO THE TEXT

Read Leviticus 11:1–16:34, noting the key words and phrases indicated below.

> *CLEAN AND UNCLEAN FOODS: God now gives instructions to Moses about which animals could be eaten and which could not.*

11:1. NOW THE LORD SPOKE TO MOSES AND AARON: Prescriptions for uncleanness are covered in this next section (Leviticus 11:1–16:34). God used the tangible issues of life, which He labeled clean or unclean, to repeatedly impress upon Israel the difference between what was holy and unholy. "Clean" means acceptable to God, while "unclean" means unacceptable to God. Leviticus 11–15 details the code of cleanness. Leviticus 16 returns to sacrifices, detailing those prescribed for the Day of Atonement.

2. THESE ARE THE ANIMALS WHICH YOU MAY EAT: This section (through verse 47) contains further legislation on the consumption of animals. Abel's offering hints at a post-Fall/pre-Flood diet of animals (see Genesis 4:4). After the Noahic flood, God specifically had granted man permission to eat meat (see 9:1–4), and here He spells out the specifics of covenant legislation. The major points were: (1) that Israel was to obey God's absolute standard, no matter what; and (2) the uniqueness of their dietary laws made it difficult for Israel to eat with the idolatrous nations around and among them, serving as a barrier to easy socialization with pagan peoples. All of the reasons for the prohibitions are not specified. Dietary and hygienic benefits were real, but only secondary to the divine purposes of teaching obedience and separation.

3. AMONG THE ANIMALS: This section (through verse 23) is repeated in Deuteronomy 14:3–20 in almost exact wording. The subject matter includes animals (Leviticus 11:3–8), water life (see verses 9–12), birds (see verses 13–19), and insects (see verses 20–23).

4. THE CAMEL: The camel has a divided foot of two large parts, but the division is not complete and the two toes rest on an elastic pad.

5–6. THE ROCK HYRAX . . . THE HARE: While not true ruminating animals, the manner in which these animals processed their food gave the distinct appearance of "chewing the cud."

9. FINS AND SCALES: Much like the cud and hoof characteristics, the "no fin and scales" guidelines ruled out a segment of water life commonly consumed by ancient people.

13. AMONG THE BIRDS: Rather than unifying characteristics as in the hoof-cud and no fin-scales descriptions, the forbidden birds were simply named.

22. THESE YOU MAY EAT: Verse 21 describes the locust, which was allowed for food.

24. BY THESE YOU SHALL BECOME UNCLEAN: This next section (through verse 43) deals with separation from other defiling things.

26–27. WHICH DIVIDES THE FOOT: These prohibited animals would include horses and donkeys, which have a single hoof, and lion and tigers, which have paws.

36. A SPRING OR A CISTERN: The movement and quantity of water determined the probability of actual contamination. Water was scarce also, and it would have been a threat to the water supply if all water touched by these prohibited carcasses were forbidden for drinking.

44–45. FOR I AM THE LORD YOUR GOD: This is the first time the statement "I am the LORD your God" is made as a reason for the required separation and holiness. After this verse, that phrase is mentioned about fifty more times in this book, along with the equally instructive claim, "I am holy."

46. THIS IS THE LAW: Because God is holy and is their God, the people are to be holy in outward ceremonial behavior as an external expression of the greater necessity of heart holiness. The connection between ceremonial holiness carries over into personal holiness. The only motivation given for all these laws is to learn to be holy because God is holy. Holiness is a theme central to Leviticus (see 10:3; 19:2; 20:7, 26; 21:6–8).

REGULATIONS FOR CHILDBIRTH: *The Lord now provides instructions for women to cleanse themselves after giving birth.*

12.2. THE DAYS OF HER CUSTOMARY IMPURITY: This refers to a woman's monthly menstruation cycle (see Leviticus 15:19–24).

3. ON THE EIGHTH DAY: Joseph and Mary followed these instructions at the birth of Christ (see Luke 2:21).

SHALL BE CIRCUMCISED: The sign of the Abrahamic Covenant (see Genesis 17:9–14) was incorporated into the laws of Mosaic cleanness. This surgery was designed to cut away the male foreskin, which could carry infections and diseases in its folds and could, therefore, pass the disease on to wives. It was important for the preservation of God's people physically. But this cleansing of the physical organ was symbolic of the deep need for the heart's cleansing from depravity, sin's deadly disease, which is most clearly revealed by procreation, as men produce sinners and only sinners. God offers this cleansing to the faithful and penitent through the sacrifice of Christ to come, which alone enables them to live devoted to God in truth faith and obedience.

6. BURNT OFFERING . . . SIN OFFERING: Though the occasion was joyous, these required sacrifices were to impress upon the parents the reality of original sin and that their child had inherited a sin nature.

8. TWO TURTLEDOVES OR TWO YOUNG PIGEONS: See Leviticus 1:14–17; 5:7–10. These were Joseph and Mary's offerings after Christ's birth (see Luke 2:24), when they presented Jesus as their firstborn to the Lord (see Exodus 13:2; Luke 2:22). Sacrificing birds, rather than livestock, indicated a low economic situation, though one who was in total poverty could offer flour (see Leviticus 5:11–13).

> REGULATIONS FOR DISEASE: *In this section, the Lord provides instructions for identifying when a person had become unclean because of a physical condition, and how that person could become ritually clean once again.*

13:2: ON THE SKIN OF HIS BODY: This section (through Leviticus 14:57) covers laws pertaining to skin diseases.

A BRIGHT SPOT: This probably refers to inflammation.

A LEPROUS SORE: This is a term referring to various ancient skin disorders that were sometimes superficial, sometimes serious. It may have included modern leprosy (Hansen's disease). The symptoms described in verses 2, 6, 10, 18, 30, and 39 are not sufficient for a diagnosis of the clinical condition. For the protection of the people, observation and isolation were demanded for all suspected cases of what could be a contagious disease.

3. IF THE HAIR ON THE SORE HAS TURNED WHITE: This biblical leprosy involved some whiteness (see Exodus 4:6), which disfigured its victim but did not disable him. Later, we read that Naaman was able to exercise his functions as

general of Syria's army, although a leper (see 2 Kings 5:1, 27). Both Old Testament and New Testament lepers went almost everywhere, indicating that this disease was not the leprosy of today that cripples a person.

12. IF LEPROSY BREAKS OUT ALL OVER THE SKIN: A victim of the scaly disease was unclean as long as the infection was partial. Once the body was covered with it, he was clean and could enter the place of worship (see through verse 17). Apparently the complete covering meant the contagious period was over.

18. IF THE BODY DEVELOPS A BOIL: The allusion to a boil (see through verse 28) with inflamed or raw areas and whitened hairs may refer to a related infection that was contagious. When lepers were cured by Christ, they were neither lame nor deformed. They were never brought on beds.

29–44. IF A MAN OR WOMAN: Similar skin conditions are described in verses 29–37 and verses 38–44 (some inflammation from infection). The aim of these laws was to protect the people from disease, but more importantly, to inculcate into them by vivid object lessons how God desired purity, holiness, and cleanness among His people.

45. UNCLEAN! UNCLEAN! Here are the symbols of grief and isolation. This same cry is later heard from the survivors of Jerusalem's destruction (see Lamentations 4:15).

47–59. IF A GARMENT HAS A LEPROUS PLAGUE IN IT: This next section deals with garments worn by infected persons.

59. TO PRONOUNCE IT CLEAN OR . . . UNCLEAN: The primary purpose of this legislation was to assist the priest in determining the presence of contagious skin disease. The language of the passage indicates disease that affects the clothes as it did the person. This provided more illustrations of the devastating infection of sin and how essential spiritual cleansing was.

14:2. THE LAW OF THE LEPER: This next section (through verse 32) explains the cleansing ritual for healed persons. It is a prescription, not for the healing itself from leprosy and other such diseases, but for the ceremonial cleansing which needed to be performed after the person was declared clean.

3. OUT OF THE CAMP: The leper was not allowed to return to society immediately. Before the person could enter the camp, some priest skilled in the diagnosis of disease needed to examine him and assist with the ritual of the two birds (see verses 4–7).

4. TWO LIVING AND CLEAN BIRDS, CEDAR WOOD, SCARLET, AND HYSSOP: The bundle of cedar and hyssop tied with scarlet included the living bird. It was all

dipped seven times into the blood of the killed bird mixed with water to symbolize purification. The bird was then set free to symbolize the leper's release from quarantine. Certain identification of hyssop is impossible, but it could be the marjoram plant.

8. OUTSIDE HIS TENT: The movement was progressive until finally he could enter and dwell in his own tent, giving dramatic indication of the importance of thorough cleansing for fellowship with God's people. This was a powerful lesson from God on the holiness He desired for those who lived among His people. That has not changed (see 2 Corinthians 7:1).

10. ON THE EIGHTH DAY: As part of the leper's ceremonial cleansing ritual, trespass offerings (see Leviticus 5:14–6:7), sin offerings (see 4:1–5:13), burnt offerings (see 1:3–17), and grain offerings (see 2:1–16) were to be made.

ONE LOG OF OIL: Less than one pint.

18. PUT ON THE HEAD: This would not have been understood as an anointing for entry into an office, but rather a symbolic gesture of cleansing and healing. There could be a connection with the New Testament directive to anoint the sick for healing (see Mark 6:13; 16:18; James 5:14).

34. I PUT THE LEPROUS PLAGUE: This next section (through verse 57) covers contaminated houses, which most likely involved some kinds of infectious bacteria, fungus, or mold. God's sovereign hand is acknowledged in the diseases that were in "the land of Canaan" (see Exodus 4:11; Deuteronomy 32:39). He had His purposes for these afflictions, as He always does. Uniquely, in Israel's case, they allowed for object lessons on holiness.

37. INGRAINED STREAKS, GREENISH OR REDDISH: The disease would appear to be some sort of contagious mildew. Leprosy (Hansen's disease), as we know it today, is not the problem here since that is a disease related to the human senses—that is, the destruction of feeling due to the dysfunction of the nerves. It is not known to be contagious either, and it couldn't be developed in a house.

38–53. THE PRIEST SHALL: The matter of cleansing such houses is now delineated.

57. TO TEACH WHEN IT IS UNCLEAN AND WHEN IT IS CLEAN: The priest needed instruction in identifying and prescribing the course for disease such as that described herein, so as to teach people the importance of distinguishing holy things.

15:2. A DISCHARGE FROM HIS BODY: This section (through Leviticus 15:33) deals with purification for bodily discharges. Several types of discharges by men (see verses 2–18) and women (see verses 19–30) are identified and given prescribed treatment.

2–18. WHEN ANY MAN: These verses describe secretions related to some disease of the male sexual organs. After he became well, he was required to make both a sin and a burnt offering (see verse 15).

16–18. UNCLEAN UNTIL EVENING: These verses refer to natural sexual gland secretions, for which no offerings were required.

19–24. IF A WOMAN: These verses concern the natural menstrual discharge of a woman, for which no offerings were required.

25–30. DISCHARGE OF BLOOD FOR MANY DAYS: These verses deal with some secretion of blood indicating disease, not menstruation, requiring a sin and burnt offering after she is well.

31. SEPARATE THE CHILDREN OF ISRAEL FROM THEIR UNCLEANNESS: In all these instructions, God was showing the Israelites that they must have a profound reverence for holy things, and nothing was more suited to that purpose than to bar from the tabernacle all who were polluted by any kind of uncleanness (ceremonial, natural, physical, or spiritual). In order to mark out His people as dwelling before Him in holiness, God required of them complete purity and didn't allow them to come before Him when defiled, even by involuntary or secret impurities.

32. THIS IS THE LAW: When one considers that God was training a people to live in His presence, it becomes apparent that these rules for the maintenance of personal purity, pointing to the necessity of purity in the heart, were neither too stringent nor too minute.

THE DAY OF ATONEMENT: In this section, the Lord instructs Moses on how the Israelites should observe this high holy day each year.

16:1. THE LORD SPOKE TO MOSES: This next section (verses 1–34) covers the Day of Atonement, which was commanded to be observed annually to cover the sins of the nation, both corporately and individually. Even with the most scrupulous observance of the required sacrifices, many sins and defilements still remained unacknowledged and, therefore, without specific expiation. This special inclusive sacrifice provided that atonement, but only those who were genuine in faith and repentance could receive its benefit: the forgiveness of God. This holiest of all Israel's festivals occurred in September/October on the tenth day of the seventh month (see verse 29). It anticipated the ultimate High Priest and the perfect sacrificial Lamb.

THE DEATH OF THE TWO SONS OF AARON: See Leviticus 10:1–3.

2. NOT TO COME AT JUST ANY TIME INTO THE HOLY PLACE: Common priests went every day to burn incense on the golden altar in the part of the tabernacle sanctuary outside the veil, where the lampstand, table, and showbread were located. None except the high priest was allowed to enter inside the veil (see verse 12), into the Holy Place—actually called the Holy of Holies, the Most Holy (see Exodus 26:33), or the Holiest of All (see Hebrews 9:3, 8), where the Ark of the Covenant rested. This arrangement was designed to inspire a reverence for God at a time when His presence was indicated by visible symbols.

APPEAR IN THE CLOUD: This cloud was likely the smoke of the incense, which the high priest burned on his annual entrance into the Most Holy Place. It was this cloud that covered the mercy seat on the Ark of the Covenant (see Leviticus 16:13).

THE MERCY SEAT: See Exodus 25:17–22. It literally means "place of atonement" and referred to the throne of God between the cherubim (see Isaiah 6). It is so named because it was where God manifested Himself for the purpose of atonement.

3. A YOUNG BULL . . . A RAM: The bull was sacrificed first as a sin offering (see Leviticus 16:11–14) and later the ram was sacrificed as a burnt offering (see verses 15–24).

4. HOLY GARMENTS: For a description of the priests' normal clothing, see Exodus 28:1–43 and Leviticus 8:6–13. The priest wore them later for the burnt offering (see 16:24). These humbler clothes were less ornate, required for the Day of Atonement to portray the high priest as God's humble servant, himself in need of atonement (see verses 11–14).

5. TWO KIDS OF THE GOATS: One animal would be killed to picture substitutionary death and the other—the scapegoat—was sent to the wilderness to represent removal of sin (see verses 7–10, 20–22).

ONE RAM: Along with the high priest's ram (see verse 3), these were to be offered as burnt offerings (see verse 24).

6. AARON SHALL OFFER THE BULL AS A SIN OFFERING: The following sequence (covered in verses 6–13) describes the activities of the high priest and those who assisted him on the Day of Atonement. First, the high priest washed at the laver in the courtyard and dressed in the tabernacle (see verse 4).

The high priest then offered the bull as a sin offering for himself and his family (see verses 3, 11).

12. BRING IT INSIDE THE VEIL: The high priest then entered the Holy of Holies with the bull's blood, incense, and burning coals from the altar of burnt offering. The veil separated all from the holy and consuming presence of God. It was this veil in Herod's temple that was torn open from top to bottom at the death of Christ, signifying a believer's access into God's presence through Jesus Christ (see Matthew 27:51; Mark 15:38; Luke 23:45).

13. ON THE TESTIMONY: The Testimony included the tablets of stone, upon which were written the Ten Commandments (Exodus 25:16; 31:18), located in the ark under the mercy seat.

14–15. SPRINKLE IT . . . KILL THE GOAT . . . SPRINKLE: The high priest sprinkled the bull's blood on the mercy seat seven times (a number that symbolically indicated completion or perfection), and then went back to the courtyard and cast lots for the two goats (see Leviticus 16:7–8). He sacrificed one goat as a sin offering for the people (see verses 5, 9, 15) and reentered the Holy of Holies to sprinkle its blood on the mercy seat and also the Holy Place (see Exodus 30:10).

16. ATONEMENT FOR THE HOLY PLACE: The object of this solemn ceremony was to impress the minds of the Israelites with the conviction that the whole tabernacle was stained by the sins of a guilty people. By those sins, they had forfeited the privileges of the presence of God and worship of Him, so that an atonement had to be made for their sins as the condition of God remaining with them.

17. HIMSELF . . . HOUSEHOLD . . . ASSEMBLY: The Day of Atonement was necessary for everyone since all had sinned, including the high priest.

18–19. ALTAR . . . CONSECRATE IT: The high priest then returned to the altar of burnt offering and cleansed it with the blood of the bull and goat (see Leviticus 16:11, 15).

20–22. HE SHALL BRING THE LIVE GOAT: The scapegoat— literally "Azazel"— was dispatched to the wilderness. Afterward, the goatkeeper cleansed himself (see verse 26).

LAY BOTH HIS HANDS ON THE HEAD: This act was more than a symbolic gesture. This "sin offering for atonement" (Numbers 29:11) was a picture of the ultimate substitutionary atonement fulfilled by the Lord Jesus Christ (see Isaiah 53:5–6; 10, 12). Jesus later fully accomplished the substitutionary bearing and total removal of sin (see Leviticus 16:22) for His people. He lived out this representation when He cried from the cross, "My God, My God, why have You forsaken Me?" (Matthew 27:46).

23–24. Aaron shall ... take off ... wash: The high priest then removed his special Day of Atonement clothing, washed again, and put on the regular high priestly clothing.

24. offer his ... and ... of the people: The high priest then offered two rams as burnt offerings for himself and the people (see Leviticus 16:3, 5).

25. The fat of the sin offering: This was then also burned.

27–28. carried outside the camp: The bull-and-goat sin offerings were carried outside the camp to be burned. This represents the historical reality of Christ's death outside of Jerusalem (see Hebrews 13:10–14). The one who burned the sin offering then cleansed himself.

29. in the seventh month: Tishri is September/October.

afflict your souls: This act of denying oneself was probably with respect to food, making the Day of Atonement the only day of prescribed fasting in Israel's annual calendar.

30. clean from all your sins: This day provided ceremonial cleansing for one year and pictured the forgiveness of God available to all who believed and repented (see Isaiah 38:17; Micah 7:19). Actual atonement was based on cleansing through the sacrifice of Christ (see Romans 3:25–26; Hebrews 9:15).

34. once a year: The better sacrifice of Jesus Christ was offered once for all, never to be repeated (see Hebrews 9:11–10:18). Upon that sacrifice all forgiveness of sin is based, including that of Old Testament believers.

Unleashing the Text

1) Why was God so particular about the minute details of His people's lives, like the kinds of foods they could eat?

_____

_____

_____

_____

_____

_____

_____

_____

2) How did the cleansing regulations regarding the birth of a child reinforce God's holiness and the uniqueness of His people?

_____

_____

_____

_____

_____

3) How would you describe the regulations concerning those with various skin diseases?

_____

_____

_____

_____

_____

4) How would the physical/medical regulations provided in Leviticus 12–15 have benefitted Israel as a community?

_____

_____

_____

_____

_____

EXPLORING THE MEANING

The dietary regulations were not really about diet. Most people know Jews practice extensive dietary and other restrictions, even if we don't know all the specifics. Yet it is important to understand God's true purpose behind the regulations He gave Israel.

Scholars have posited various reasons, such as health and hygiene. For example, some have cited the possible danger of contracting disease after eating undercooked pork. Others have looked for a spiritual angle, suggesting that certain animals were off limits because they were connected to pagan ritual or death, like carrion eaters or animals that crawled on the ground like the serpent from the garden of Eden.

There may be some validity to those connections. However, Scripture itself gives us the reasons for God's dietary restrictions: God was teaching His people to live antithetically—different to the surrounding idolatrous peoples, and even to their own instincts or tendencies. The Lord did not say, "You shall not eat these things because they are unhealthy." Rather, He said, "You shall not make yourselves abominable with any creeping thing that creeps; nor shall you make yourselves unclean with them, lest you be defiled by them. For I am the LORD your God. . . . Neither shall you defile yourselves with any creeping thing that creeps on the earth. For I am the LORD who brings you up out of the land of Egypt, to be your God. You shall therefore be holy, for I am holy" (Leviticus 11:43–45).

God's dietary restrictions were training in *holiness*. He wanted the Israelites to be set apart from the rest of the peoples of the earth. He wanted them to look different, act different, and even eat different. He wanted them to be holy, as He is holy.

To be "clean" wasn't really about cleanliness. In addition to certain animals being clean or unclean, several chapters in Leviticus describe situations, ailments, or physical conditions that could make a person clean or unclean. For example: "If a woman has conceived, and borne a male child, then she shall be unclean seven days; as in the days of her customary impurity she shall be unclean" (12:2). Or, "If a man or a woman has bright spots on the skin of the body, specifically white bright spots, then the priest shall look; and indeed if the bright spots on the skin of the body are dull white, it is a white spot that grows on the skin. He is clean" (13:38–39).

As with the dietary restrictions in Leviticus 11, there were some practical benefits to God's regulations about when a person would be clean or unclean. If an Israelite had a contagious skin disease, for example, it was helpful for the overall health of the community to have that person quarantined (declared unclean) until the ailment was no longer an issue.

However, as with the dietary restrictions, the primary motivator for these personal guidelines was to remind the Israelites of their need for personal holiness and purity. God used clean and unclean distinctions to separate Israel nationally, illustrating that His people must learn to live His way—in everything.

His regulations emphasized how crucial obedience is by teaching His people how to obey Him in every mundane area of life. Sacrifices, rituals, diet, and even clothing and cooking were all carefully ordered by God to teach Israel that they were to live differently from everyone else; the regulations were an external illustration of the separation from sin God's people were to practice in their hearts. Because the Lord is their God, they were to be utterly distinct.

Physical cleanliness was never as important as spiritual cleanliness. At one point during Jesus' ministry, He confronted the Pharisees for their continual emphasis on outward cleanliness, even as they ignored their spiritual corruption. "Now you Pharisees make the outside of the cup and dish clean, but your inward part is full of greed and wickedness. Foolish ones! Did not He who made the outside make the inside also?" (Luke 11:39–40). "There is nothing that enters a man from outside which can defile him; but the things which come out of him, those are the things that defile a man" (Mark 7:15).

The Pharisees, of course, were deeply familiar with the dietary restrictions and purity laws that are recorded in the book Leviticus. They made certain to follow those laws to the letter. Yet in the process, they lost sight of the truth that God's instructions for purity were meant to highlight every person's need for holiness—"through the Law comes knowledge of sin" (Romans 3:20, NASB).

Even today, it is easy for us to focus on the external elements of what people understand to be Christianity: going to church, tithing, doing good things; and not doing bad things such as cursing, stealing, lying, and so on. Obviously, God's people should demonstrate righteousness. Yet we must never forget that outward actions have never been the end goal. God has always been after our spiritual condition. He wants us to be perfectly holy, as He is holy.

REFLECTING ON THE TEXT

5) In what ways are Christians supposed to be set apart from the rest of the world today?

_____

_____

_____

_____

_____

_____

6) What are some practical steps you can take to separate yourself from the world's corrupting influence?

_____

_____

_____

_____

7) What are some religious traditions and rituals that people often use today to portray themselves as being "clean"?

_____

_____

_____

_____

8) When have you felt spiritually unclean? What did you do in response?

_____

_____

_____

_____

PERSONAL RESPONSE

9) What are some practices or habits you use to display a merely external appearance of holiness?

_____

_____

_____

_____

_____

10) What steps can you take to discontinue those practices and habits? What can you do instead to cultivate true holiness?

_____

_____

_____

_____

_____

4

MANDATES FOR HOLINESS
Leviticus 17:1–20:27

DRAWING NEAR

What do the laws of your community tell you about the people who live in that community?

_____

_____

_____

_____

_____

_____

THE CONTEXT

One thing to remember about the book of Leviticus is that all the action occurs in a single place: at the base of Mount Sinai. Whereas Exodus records the Israelites' harrowing journey from Egypt through the Red Sea and ultimately to Sinai, Leviticus has no geographical movement. Everything happens in the same place over a relative short period of time in 1145 BC.

The chapters we will cover in this lesson offer further laws and regulations for God's people. These laws were revealed by God to Moses while the people camped at the base of the Mount Sinai. Specifically, we will explore God's establishment of the Day of Atonement—a notable day in the Jewish calendar. We will also highlight some of the criminal codes God handed down to Moses, as well as regulations on sexual practices and other issues of morality.

KEYS TO THE TEXT

Read Leviticus 17:1–20:27, noting the key words and phrases indicated below.

> LAWS FOR GOD'S PEOPLE: *The Lord provides mandates for practical holiness, which include specific laws pertaining to sacrifice, purity, and neighborliness.*

17:3. OUTSIDE THE CAMP: In this section (verses 1–9), the Lord warns against sacrificing anywhere other than at the door of the tabernacle of meeting.

4. GUILT OF BLOODSHED: An unauthorized sacrifice could result in death.

10. WHO EATS ANY BLOOD: Warnings against the misuse of blood are issued in this next section (through verse 16; see 7:26–27; also Deuteronomy 12:16, 23–25; 15:23; 1 Samuel 14:32–34).

11. LIFE OF THE FLESH IS IN THE BLOOD: This phrase is amplified by "its blood sustains its life" (Leviticus 17:14). Blood carries life-sustaining elements to all parts of the body; therefore, it represents the essence of life. In contrast, the shedding of blood represents the shedding of life; that is, death (see Genesis 9:4). New Testament references to the shedding of the blood of Jesus Christ are references to His death.

BLOOD THAT MAKES ATONEMENT: Since blood contains the life, it is sacred to God. Shed blood (death) from a substitute atones for or covers the sinner, who is then allowed to live.

13–14. THE STRANGERS WHO DWELL AMONG YOU: It was customary with heathen hunters, when they killed any game, to pour out the blood as an offering to the god of the hunt. The Israelites, to the contrary, were enjoined by this directive and banned from all such superstitious acts of idolatry.

15–16. WASH HIS CLOTHES AND BATHE: This cleansing was necessary because these animals would not have had the blood drained properly (see Exodus 22:31; Deuteronomy 14:21).

> LAWS FOR PROPER SEXUAL BEHAVIOR: *The Lord provides mandates related to sexual practices, which would eliminate the abominations that were being practiced by the heathen in the land.*

18:1–30. These laws assume the general prohibition of adultery (see Exodus 20:14) and a father incestuously engaging his daughter. They do not necessarily invalidate the special case of a levirate marriage (see Deuteronomy 25:5). The penalties for such outlawed behavior are detailed in Leviticus 20:10–21.

3. DOINGS OF THE LAND: Repeating the sexual practices or customs of the Egyptians and Canaanites was forbidden by God.

4. I AM THE LORD YOUR GOD. This phrase, used over fifty times, asserts the uniqueness of the one true and living God, who calls His people to holiness as He is holy, and calls them to reject all other gods.

5. IF A MAN DOES, HE SHALL LIVE BY THEM: Special blessing was promised to the Israelites on the condition of their obedience to God's law. This promise was remarkably verified in particular eras of their history, in the national prosperity they enjoyed when pure and undefiled religion prevailed among them. Obedience to God's Law always ensures temporal blessings, as this verse indicates. But these words have a higher reference to spiritual life as indicated by the Lord (see Luke 10:28) and by the apostle Paul (see Romans 10:5). Obedience does not save from sin and hell, but it does mark those who are saved (see Ephesians 2:8–9).

6–18. This section deals with consanguinity, i.e., the sins of incest.

6. UNCOVER HIS NAKEDNESS: This is a euphemism for sexual relations.

8. YOUR FATHER'S WIFE. Actually, a stepmother is in mind here (see verse 7).

11. YOUR SISTER: Here, he is forbidden to marry a stepsister.

18. WHILE THE OTHER IS ALIVE: The principle on which the prohibitions are made changes slightly. Instead of avoiding sexual involvement because it would violate a relational connection, this situation defaults to the principle of one person at a time, or while the other is still alive, i.e., it forbids polygamy. Commonly in Egyptian, Chaldean, and Canaanite culture, sisters were taken as wives in polygamous unions. God forbids such, as all polygamy is forbidden by the original law of marriage (see Genesis 2:24–25). Moses, because of hard hearts, tolerated it, as did others in Israel in the early stages of that nation. But it always led to tragedy.

19. CUSTOMARY IMPURITY: This refers to a woman's menstrual period (see 15:24).

21. MOLECH: This Semitic false deity (god of the Ammonites) was worshiped with child sacrifice (see Leviticus 20:2–5; 1 Kings 11:7; 2 Kings 23:10; Jeremiah 32:35). Since this chapter deals otherwise with sexual deviation, there is likely an unmentioned sexual perversion connected with this pagan ritual. Jews giving false gods homage gave foreigners occasion to blaspheme the true God.

22. NOT LIE WITH A MALE: This outlaws all homosexuality (see Leviticus 20:13; Romans 1:27; 1 Corinthians 6:9; 1 Timothy 1:10).

23. MATE WITH ANY ANIMAL: This outlaws the sexual perversion of bestiality.

29. CUT OFF: All the sexual perversions discussed in this chapter were worthy of death, indicating their loathsomeness before God.

30. WERE COMMITTED BEFORE YOU: Not in their presence, but by the people who inhabited the land before them in time (see verse 27), were such sins committed.

LAWS FOR NEIGHBORLINESS: *Here the Lord provides the practical applications of holy conduct in society.*

19:2. I THE LORD YOUR GOD AM HOLY: This basic statement, which gives the reason for holy living among God's people, is the central theme in Leviticus (see 20:26). Israel had been called to be a holy nation, and the perfectly holy character of God (see Isaiah 6:3) was the model after which the Israelites were to live (see Leviticus 10:3; 20:26; 21:6–8).

3. REVERE HIS MOTHER AND HIS FATHER: The fifth commandment (see Exodus 20:12) to honor one's father and mother is amplified by the use of a different word, "revere." Because they revered (an attitude), they could then honor (an action).

4. DO NOT TURN TO IDOLS: In addition to the fifth commandment, the fourth (see Leviticus 19:3), the first (see verse 4), and the second (see verse 4) were commanded as illustrations of holy behavior (see Exodus 20:3–6, 8–11).

9–10. WHEN YOU REAP: This was the law of gleaning (see Leviticus 23:22; Deuteronomy 24:19–22), a practice seen in Ruth 2:8–23.

11–12. YOU SHALL NOT STEAL ... DEAL FALSELY ... LIE TO ONE ANOTHER ... SWEAR BY MY NAME FALSELY ... PROFANE THE NAME OF YOUR GOD: Commandments from Exodus 20 are again repeated.

13. WAGES ... SHALL NOT REMAIN WITH YOU ALL NIGHT: Hired workers were to be paid at the end of a work day. Unsalaried day workers depended on pay each day for their sustenance.

14. THE DEAF ... THE BLIND: The God of compassion has always demonstrated a concern for the disabled.

16. TAKE A STAND AGAINST THE LIFE: This refers to doing anything that would wrongfully jeopardize the life of a neighbor.

18. YOU SHALL LOVE YOUR NEIGHBOR AS YOURSELF: This, which Jesus called the second great commandment, is the most often quoted Old Testament text in the New Testament (see Matthew 5:43; 19:19; 22:39; Mark 12:31, 33; Luke 10:27; Romans 13:9; Galatians 5:14; James 2:8).

19. WITH ANOTHER KIND . . . MIXED: These mixtures may have been characteristic of some idolatrous practices.

20–22. WHOEVER LIES CARNALLY WITH A WOMAN . . . BETROTHED TO A MAN AS A CONCUBINE: In the case of immorality with a betrothed slave, the couple was to be punished (possibly by scourging), but not killed. Afterward, a trespass offering was to be rendered with appropriate reparation. This is an exception to the norm (see Deuteronomy 22:23–24).

23. COUNT THEIR FRUIT AS UNCIRCUMCISED: The Israelites could not eat from the fruit trees of Canaan for four years after entering the land because the fruit of the first three years was to be considered unclean, and the fourth year the fruit was to be offered to the Lord. Some gardeners say preventing a tree from bearing fruit in the first years, by cutting off the blossoms, makes it more productive.

26. DIVINATION OR SOOTHSAYING: Attempting to tell the future with the help of snakes and clouds was a common ancient way of foretelling good or bad future. These were forbidden forms of witchcraft which involved demonic activity.

27–28. SHAVE AROUND . . . YOUR HEAD . . . BEARD . . . CUTTINGS IN YOUR FLESH: These pagan practices were most likely associated with Egyptian idolatry and were therefore to be avoided. It was universal practice among pagans, in times of grief, to make deep gashes on the face and arms or legs. It was seen as a mark of respect for the dead, as well as a sort of propitiatory offering to the gods who presided over death. The Jews learned this custom in Egypt and, though weaned from it, relapsed into the old superstition (see Isaiah 22:12; Jeremiah 16:6; 47:5).

TATTOO ANY MARKS: Tattoos were connected to names of idols and were permanent signs of apostasy.

29. PROSTITUTE YOUR DAUGHTER: Even the pagans of ancient Assyria at this time forbade such horrendous means of monetary gain.

31. MEDIUMS AND FAMILIAR SPIRITS: Mediums are humans who act as go-betweens to supposedly contact/communicate with the spirits of the dead, who are actually impersonated by demons. "Familiar spirits" refers to demons.

32. RISE BEFORE THE GRAY HEADED: Showing respect for the older man acknowledged God's blessing of long life and the wisdom that comes with it (see Isaiah 3:5).

36. EPHAH . . . HIN: These dry and liquid measures, respectively, were approximately equal to four to six gallons and six to eight pints.

THE CONSEQUENCES: *The Lord concludes by naming grave punishments for those who chose to violate His laws within the Israelite community.*

20:1. THE LORD SPOKE TO MOSES: Capital and other grave crimes are discussed in this section (through Leviticus 20:27). Many of the same issues from Leviticus 18 and 19 are elaborated, with the emphasis here on the penalty paid for the violation.

2. GIVES ANY OF HIS DESCENDANTS TO MOLECH: Molech (or Moloch), the Ammonite god of the people surrounding Israel, required human (especially child) sacrifice (see Leviticus 20:2–5; Jeremiah 32:35). There was also likely an unmentioned sexual perversion connected with this pagan ritual, hence its prohibition in Leviticus 18 also. Jews giving false gods homage gave foreigners occasion to blaspheme the true God.

5. PROSTITUTE THEMSELVES: This speaks figuratively of spiritual harlotry.

5–6. CUT HIM OFF: This means to kill. It is synonymous with "put to death" in verse 9.

9. CURSES HIS FATHER OR HIS MOTHER: Doing the very opposite of the commands to honor and revere (see 19:3) had fatal consequences. (See Mark 7:10, where Jesus referred to this text.)

10–21. THE MAN WHO COMMITS: This section gives the punishments for violating the prohibitions of sexual sins detailed in Leviticus 18:1–30 (see also Deuteronomy 22:13–30).

22. MAY NOT VOMIT YOU OUT: God repeatedly told Israel that remaining in the land required obedience to the Mosaic Covenant (see Leviticus 18:25, 28).

UNLEASHING THE TEXT

1) How would you describe the events that took place on the Day of Atonement?

---

2) What role did the scapegoat play in the Day of Atonement ceremonies?

_____

_____

_____

_____

_____

3) Do the laws regarding sexual immorality in Leviticus 18 apply today? Explain.

_____

_____

_____

_____

_____

4) What were the consequences for violating God's laws as outlined in Leviticus 20?

_____

_____

_____

_____

_____

EXPLORING THE MEANING

The Day of Atonement foreshadowed the atoning work of Christ. Leviticus 16 contains instructions for the Day of Atonement, which was to be observed each year by God's people. The purpose of this day was both simple and profound: "For on that day the priest shall make atonement for you, to cleanse you, that you may be clean from all your sins before the LORD" (verse 30).

The ceremony for the Day of Atonement is rich and filled with powerful imagery. The high priest's duties on that day foreshadowed Jesus' sacrifice on the cross. For example, only the high priest was allowed to enter the inner portion of the tabernacle, commonly called the Holy of Holies. But to do so, the priest was required to work through a staggering list of bathings, cleansings, and sacrifices—simply to walk through the door into the Most Holy place. This served as both a picture of and a contrast to Jesus, who as the perfect High Priest is the only one able to make atonement for sin, yet who has continual and unfettered access to the throne room of heaven because He Himself is God.

The Day of Atonement also involved two goats, whose respective fates were determined by God through casting lots (verse 8). The first goat was sacrificed within the tabernacle: "He shall kill the goat of the sin offering, which is for the people, bring its blood inside the veil . . . and sprinkle it on the mercy seat and before the mercy seat. So he shall make atonement . . . because of the uncleanness of the children of Israel, and because of their transgressions, for all their sins" (verses 15–16). The second goat was brought alive into the courtyard of the tabernacle. What happened next is a poignant visual: "Aaron shall lay both his hands on the head of the live goat, confess over it all the iniquities of the children of Israel, and all their transgressions, concerning all their sins, putting them on the head of the goat, and shall send it away into the wilderness . . . . The goat shall bear on itself all their iniquities to an uninhabited land" (verses 21–22). Like these goats, Jesus was killed on the mountain of God to make atonement for sin, and He carried away our sins on His body at the moment of His death. But unlike the Day of Atonement, Jesus' sacrifice made atonement once for all.

God's regulations for purity were deeply personal. It is common in today's culture for people to elevate personal privacy as a supreme and inviolable virtue. We are often told that whatever people do in their own homes is solely their business, as long as they are not harming anyone else. These beliefs are typically couched as valuing personal freedom.

However, when you read through Leviticus 18, it becomes clear that God does not subscribe to the idea that individual privacy is sacrosanct. Instead, God rightly extended *His* sovereignty and authority into the most private areas of His people's lives. God commanded the Israelites to avoid specific romantic relations. He labeled specific sexual practices as "wickedness" (verse 17), "abomination" (verse 22), "perversion" (verse 23), and more. He again condemned idolatry and even required the Israelites to "cut off" (verse 29)—that is, kill—any member of the community who violated His commands, even in private.

It may be tempting to view God's commands in this chapter of Leviticus as overly restrictive or an overreach against personal freedoms. In reality, God in rightful exercise of His authority was providing the Israelites with helpful boundaries so they could avoid defiling themselves and their neighbors through sinning. In other words, God was granting His people true freedom—the freedom to be holy as He is holy.

God was showing that He and His people were distinctly holy. It is important to remember that the Israelites were surrounded by polytheistic cultures; each of their neighbors was deeply enmeshed in the worship of—typically multiple—false gods. Such was the culture of their world.

God's regulations in Leviticus (and elsewhere in Scripture) were His gracious guidelines to help His people avoid assimilating into that culture. God desired His chosen people to create a new and distinct culture—one based on holiness. The beginning of Leviticus 18 reveals that priority: "Then the LORD spoke to Moses, saying, 'Speak to the children of Israel, and say to them: "I am the LORD your God. According to the doings of the land of Egypt, where you dwelt, you shall not do; and according to the doings of the land of Canaan, where I am bringing you, you shall not do; nor shall you walk in their ordinances. You shall observe My judgments and keep My ordinances, to walk in them: I am the LORD your God"'" (verses 1–4).

Again, at the beginning of Leviticus 19, God says, "Speak to all the congregation of the children of Israel, and say to them: 'You shall be holy, for I the LORD your God am holy'" (verse 2). God wanted His people to be set apart from the world—to be holy as He is holy, so that they might experience true life (see 18:5).

REFLECTING ON THE TEXT

5) What are some similarities between the Day of Atonement and Christ's sacrifice on the cross?

_____

_____

_____

_____

_____

6) How do the rigorous regulations for the Day of Atonement emphasize the severity of Christ's sacrifice?

_____

_____

_____

_____

_____

7) Why did God want His people to be set apart from the other cultures of the day?

_____

_____

_____

_____

_____

8) What are some ways to stand for truth and obey God's commands in today's society?

_____

_____

_____

_____

_____

PERSONAL RESPONSE

9) What part does the confession of sin play in your spiritual life? What practical steps are you taking to put off sin?

_____

_____

_____

_____

_____

_____

10) How will you seek to be holy as God is holy?

_____

_____

_____

_____

_____

_____

5

FEASTS AND FESTIVALS

Leviticus 21:1–27:34

DRAWING NEAR

What are some of your family's traditions that remind you of God's faithfulness?

_____

_____

_____

_____

_____

_____

_____

_____

THE CONTEXT

When readers of Scripture encounter the book of Leviticus, they often get a bit lost in the details of the laws, rules, and regulations that God prescribed to his people. And there are certainly a lot of commands within this book. Commands about offerings and sacrifices. Commands about food and diet. Commands about cleanliness and dealing with illnesses. Commands pertaining to just about every aspect of everyday life.

However, as we have seen throughout this study, the goal of these laws was not to restrict God's people or curtail their freedoms. Instead, the purpose behind the Lord's laws was to help His people live in holiness—to keep them distinct as belonging to Him, set apart from the pagan and immoral practices of the peoples around them. This included Egypt (the country the Lord freed them from) and Canaan (the new homeland the Lord was giving to them).

In this lesson, we will conclude our study on Leviticus and prepare to engage the book of Deuteronomy. As we explore these final chapters in Leviticus, we will see God's continued requirement for holiness among His priests, the establishment of several feasts and holy days, and God's celebration of rest and freedom through sabbatical years and the year of jubilee.

KEYS TO THE TEXT
Read Leviticus 21:1–27:34, noting the key words and phrases indicated below.

> INSTRUCTIONS FOR THE PRIESTS: *To serve the Lord God as a priest demanded a higher standard of holy conduct than for the general Israelite.*

21:1. DEFILE HIMSELF FOR THE DEAD: Coming into contact with a corpse (see Numbers 19:11) or being in the same room with one (see 19:14) made one unclean. The exceptions were the dead from the priest's own family (see Leviticus 21:2–4).

6. THE BREAD OF THEIR GOD: This phrase appears five times in Leviticus 21 (verses 8, 17, 21, 22). It most likely refers to the bread of the Presence in the Holy Place (see Leviticus 24:5–9; Exodus 25:30; 39:36; 40:23).

7. HARLOT OR A DEFILED WOMAN . . . DIVORCED: The priest was allowed to marry, but only in the purest of circumstances (see also Leviticus 21:13–14). A holy marriage union pictured the holy union between God and His people. The priests were to be living models of that holy union. (See the apostle Paul's words regarding pastors in 1 Timothy 3:2, 4 and Titus 1:6.)

9. PROFANES HER FATHER: The priests' children were to live holy lives also. The common punishment of stoning (see Deuteronomy 22:21) is replaced with burning by fire.

10. HE WHO IS THE HIGH PRIEST: These verses (through verse 15) give a summary of the standards for the high priest, which were the highest and most holy in accord with his utmost sacred responsibility.

SHALL NOT UNCOVER HIS HEAD NOR TEAR HIS CLOTHES: These were acts associated with mourning or anguish. This law was violated at Christ's trial (see Matthew 26:65; Mark 14:63).

16–23. NO MAN ... WHO HAS ANY DEFECT: Just as the sacrifice had to be without blemish, so did the one offering the sacrifice. As visible things exert strong impressions on the minds of people, any physical impurity or malformation tended to distract from the weight and authority of the sacred office, failed to externally exemplify the inward wholeness God sought, and failed to be a picture of Jesus Christ, the perfect High Priest to come (see Hebrews 7:26).

22:2. DO NOT PROFANE MY HOLY NAME: What follows in this section (through verse 33) are additional instructions on ceremonial cleanness for the priests, beginning with a death threat in verse 3 to "cut off " those who might violate these rules.

7. WHEN THE SUN GOES DOWN HE SHALL BE CLEAN: Time was essential for ceremonial purification.

11. BUYS A PERSON: This portion of the sacrifice assigned to the support of the priests was restricted to the use of his family. However, an indentured servant was to be treated as one of the priest's family, pertaining to eating the consecrated food. See the laws of release, which show this to be a temporary indenture (see Leviticus 25:10; Exodus 21:2–11; Deuteronomy 15:12–18).

17–30. OFFERS HIS SACRIFICE: This section describes the unacceptable and acceptable sacrifices.

31–33. I WILL BE HALLOWED: The motive behind obedience to God was His holy nature and grace in delivering the nation.

> THE GREAT FEASTS OF ISRAEL: God ordains several specific days each
> year in the Israelite calendar to serve as community-wide opportunities
> to celebrate His faithfulness, remember the past, and worship Him.

23:1. THE FEASTS OF THE LORD: Holiness issues that pertain to the nation collectively are outlined in this next section (Leviticus 23:1–27:34), beginning with the special feasts that the Israelites were to observe each year (see 23:1–24:9; Exodus 23:14–17; Numbers 28:1–29:40; Deuteronomy 16:1–17). After a reminder that the Sabbath was a weekly day sacred to the Lord (see Leviticus 23:3), the feasts are given in the order of the calendar (see verses 4–44).

2. PROCLAIM TO BE HOLY CONVOCATIONS: These festivals did not involve gatherings of all Israel in every case. Only the feasts of Unleavened Bread, Weeks, and Tabernacles required that all males gather in Jerusalem (see Exodus 23:14–17; Deuteronomy 16:16–17).

3. SABBATH OF SOLEMN REST: The Mosaic ordinance of the fourth commandment came first (see Genesis 2:1–3; Exodus 20:8–11).

4–22. FEASTS OF THE LORD: Three events were commemorated in March/April: (1) Passover on the fourteenth (see Leviticus 23:5); (2) Feast of Unleavened Bread on the fifteenth to the twenty-first (see verses 6–8); and Feast of Firstfruits on the day after the Sabbath of Unleavened Bread week (see verses 9–14).

5. THE LORD'S PASSOVER: The festival commemorated God's deliverance of Israel from Egypt (see Exodus 12:1–14, 43–49; Numbers 28:16; Deuteronomy 16:1–2).

6–14. FIRSTFRUITS OF YOUR HARVEST: This festival, known as the Feast of Unleavened Bread, commemorated Israel's hurried departure from Egypt and the associated hardships (see Exodus 12:15–20; 13:3–10; Numbers 28:17–25; Deuteronomy 16:3–8). The festival dedicated the initial part of the barley harvest in March/April and was celebrated on the day after the Sabbath of Unleavened Bread week. It involved presenting to the Lord a sheaf of barley (see Leviticus 23:10–11) accompanied by burnt, grain, and drink offerings (see Exodus 29:40). Firstfruits symbolized the consecration of the whole harvest to God and was a pledge of the whole harvest to come (see Romans 8:23; 11:16; 1 Corinthians 15:20; James 1:18).

15–22. COUNT FIFTY DAYS: The Feast of Weeks (May/June) dedicated the firstfruits of the wheat harvest (see Exodus 23:16; Numbers 28:26–31; Deuteronomy 16:9–12). It occurred on the fiftieth day after the Sabbath preceding the Feast of Firstfruits. It is also known as the Feast of Harvest (see Exodus 23:16) and Pentecost, Greek for *fifty* (see Acts 2:1).

23–43. THE LORD SPOKE TO MOSES: This next section outlines three events the Israelites were to commemorate: (1) Feast of Trumpets on the first (see verses 23–25); (2) Day of Atonement on the tenth (see verses 26–32); and (3) Feast of Tabernacles on the fifteenth to the twenty-first (see verses 33–43).

23–25. MEMORIAL OF BLOWING OF TRUMPETS: This feast, called the Feast of Trumpets, consecrated the seventh month (September/October) as a sabbatical month (see Numbers 29:1–6).

26–32. DAY OF ATONEMENT: The annual Day of Atonement pointed to the forgiveness and cleansing of sin for the priests, the nation, and the tabernacle.

33–43. FEAST OF TABERNACLES: This festival commemorated God's deliverance, protection, and provision during the wilderness wanderings of the Exodus (see Exodus 23:16; Numbers 29:12–38; Deuteronomy 16:13–15).

It is also known as the Feast of Booths (see Deuteronomy 16:13) and Feast of Ingathering (see Exodus 23:16). The people lived in booths or huts made from limbs (see Nehemiah 8:14–18), remembering their wilderness experience. It also celebrated the autumn harvest and will be celebrated in the Millennium (see Zechariah 14:16).

> *CARE OF THE TABERNACLE: The Lord provides additional instructions for the tabernacle, specifically relating to the lamps and the bread.*

24:1–9. COMMAND THE CHILDREN OF ISRAEL: Instructions for the lamps (see Leviticus 24:1–4) are also outlined in Exodus 25:31–40; 27:20, 21; 37:17–24. Instructions for the bread (see Leviticus 24:5–9) are also outlined in Exodus 25:23–30; 39:36; 40:23.

5. BAKE TWELVE CAKES: Each loaf was made with four quarts of flour.

10–14, 23. NOW THE SON: This represents another historical example of blasphemy along similar lines as the account of Nadab and Abihu (see Leviticus 10:1–2). The blasphemer was one of the "many other people." The people transferred the guilt of them all to him.

12. PUT HIM IN CUSTODY: There were no jails in Israel since incarceration was not a penalty for crime. They had merely restrained him, probably in a pit of some sort, until they could establish his punishment. Punishments were corporal, banishment, or, in severe cases, death. Those who lived through the punishment worked to secure restitution for those they had violated.

20. EYE FOR EYE, TOOTH FOR TOOTH: See Matthew 5:38. This law of retaliation established the principle that the punishment should fit the crime, but not go beyond it.

> *SABBATH AND JUBILEE: God provides instructions for the sabbatical years and for a special year of freedom for His people called Jubilee.*

25:2. WHEN YOU COME INTO THE LAND: In this section, proper care for the Lord's property is prescribed for the sabbatical year (see Leviticus 25:1–7) and the Jubilee year (see verses 8–55).

1–7. BUT IN THE SEVENTH YEAR: This involves revitalization of the land. The seventh year of rest would invigorate and replenish the nutrients in the soil. Whatever grew naturally was free to all for the taking (see verses 6–7).

9. JUBILEE: This literally means "ram's horn," which was blown on the tenth day of the seventh month to start the fiftieth year of universal redemption. The Year of Jubilee involved a year of release from indebtedness (see verses 23–38) and bondage of all sorts (see verses 39–55). All prisoners and captives were set free, slaves released, and debtors absolved. All property reverted to original owners. This plan curbed inflation and moderated acquisitions. It also gave new opportunity to people who had fallen on hard times.

10. PROCLAIM LIBERTY: Not only were the people required to let the land lie fallow, but they were also allowed a one-year break from their labor. Those bound by a work contract were released from their commitments, and all indentured servants were released.

14–16. IF YOU SELL ANYTHING: The Jubilee year had an effect on the value of land, which was to be considered in all transactions.

17. YOU SHALL NOT OPPRESS ONE ANOTHER: No one should take advantage of or abuse another person, because cruelty is against the very character of God. Penalties for crime were to be swift and exact.

20–22. WE SHALL NOT SOW: God promised to provide abundantly for His people in the year of no planting, which the nation had already experienced on a smaller scale on Sabbath days during the Exodus (see Exodus 16:5).

23. THE LAND IS MINE: Various regulations regarding real estate are now outlined (through verse 34). God owns the earth and all that is in it (see Psalm 24:1). The people of Israel were, in fact, only tenants on the land by the Lord's grace. Therefore, their ownership of property was temporary, not permanent.

33. CITIES OF THE LEVITES: See Numbers 35:1–8 and Joshua 21.

34. COMMON-LAND: Fields that the village or city-at-large used to grow crops.

35. LIKE A STRANGER OR A SOJOURNER: Instructions on dealing with the poor are now outlined (through verse 38). The law required gleanings (leftovers after harvest) for the Israelite as well as the stranger (see Leviticus 19:9–10; 23:22; Deuteronomy 24:19–21).

36. USURY OR INTEREST: Usury or excessive interest was prohibited for all (see Psalm 15:5). Even fair interest was otherwise prohibited in dealing with the poor (see Deuteronomy 23:19–20; 24:10–13). The basics of life were to be given, not loaned, to the poor.

38. TO GIVE YOU THE LAND OF CANAAN: The Lord cites His generosity in giving them a land that was not theirs as a motive for their generosity toward their countrymen.

39. IF ONE OF YOUR BRETHREN . . . SELLS HIMSELF TO YOU: The principles for dealing with slavery are laid out (through verse 55).

42. FOR THEY ARE MY SERVANTS: The spirit of Old Testament slavery is revealed in these words. God, in effect, ordered that slaves be treated like family (that is, better than employees), because they are His slaves whom He redeemed out of the slave markets of Egypt. God owned not only the land (see verse 23), but also the people.

44–46. FROM THE NATIONS: These slaves included people whom Israel was to either drive out or destroy (slavery was a humane option) and those who came to Israel in the Exodus from Egypt.

47. ONE OF YOUR BRETHREN . . . SELLS HIMSELF TO THE STRANGER OR SOJOURNER: This section (through verse 55) deals with an alien who has an Israelite slave.

48. REDEEMED: Redemption, a contractual agreement which existed in the slave culture, offered the potential for emancipation to indentured individuals under certain conditions. Slaves could be bought out of slavery or some other sort of indentured status by family members or other interested parties who would pay the ransom price.

51–54. THE PRICE OF HIS REDEMPTION: The cost of buying him out of slavery was affected by the Jubilee year, when he could be set free.

55. SERVANTS TO ME: The Israelites, emancipated from Egypt by God, were all God's servants; therefore, they were to treat their own slaves with the same grace and generosity that God had granted them.

BLESSINGS AND CURSES: God outlines the covenant blessings the people would receive for obeying His laws and the curses they could expect for disobedience. A provision for repentance is also offered.

26:1–2. YOU SHALL NOT MAKE IDOLS: A representative summary of the Ten Commandments (Exodus 20:3–17) was set forth as the standard by which Israel's obedience or disobedience would be measured.

IMAGE . . . PILLAR . . . ENGRAVED STONE: Israel's neighbors used all of these components for the worship of their gods.

3. IF YOU WALK IN MY STATUTES: In this section (through Leviticus 26:13), the Lord outlines the blessings with which He would reward obedience to His laws.

4. RAIN IN ITS SEASON: If the rains did not come at the right times, the people experienced crop failure and famine (see 1 Kings 17, 18).

6. EVIL BEASTS: Dangerous animals such as lions and bears existed in that area. Joseph's brothers had claimed that such an animal had killed him (see Genesis 37:20).

7. CHASE YOUR ENEMIES: God provided victories repeatedly in the conquest of Canaan (see Joshua 8–12).

9. MAKE YOU FRUITFUL, MULTIPLY YOU AND CONFIRM MY COVENANT WITH YOU: What God commanded at Creation and repeated after the Flood was contained in the covenant promise of seed (see Genesis 12:1–3), which He will fulfill to the nation of Israel as promised to Abraham (see 15:5–6).

12. YOUR GOD . . . MY PEOPLE: The promise of an intimate covenant relationship with the God of the universe is given (see 2 Corinthians 6:16).

14. BUT IF YOU DO NOT OBEY ME: In this section (through Leviticus 26:39), the Lord outlines the punishments that will accompany disobedience to His laws.

15. BREAK MY COVENANT: By disobeying the commandments and the various laws of the Mosaic Covenant, Israel broke this conditional covenant. Unlike the ultimate provisions of the unconditional covenant made with Abraham, all blessings in the covenant of Mosaic law were conditioned upon obedience (see verses 18–21).

16. WASTING DISEASE: Perhaps tuberculosis or leprosy is in view (the subject of much legislation in Leviticus 13–14), but no certain identification here is possible.

YOUR ENEMIES SHALL EAT IT: They will be conquered by their enemies at a time when those enemies will enjoy Israel's harvest.

22. HIGHWAYS SHALL BE DESOLATE: The activity on a nation's roadway—messengers, merchants, people traveling—reflected the well-being of that country. This is a picture of extreme economic siege.

25. THE VENGEANCE OF THE COVENANT: God's retribution for Israel's breaking the conditional Mosaic Covenant is pledged.

29. EAT THE FLESH: There would be widespread famine in the land and, thus, the people would even resort to cannibalism. This actually came to pass (see 2 Kings 6:28–29; Jeremiah 19:9; Lamentations 2:20; 4:10).

30. HIGH PLACES: These were natural shrines for the worship of idols. Solomon disobeyed God by worshiping Him on the high places (see 1 Kings

3:4), and not long afterward, he was serving the gods of his foreign wives (see 11:1–9).

31–35. LAY YOUR CITIES WASTE: All this occurred during the terrible invasion of the northern kingdom of Israel in 722 BC by the Assyrians and the destruction of the southern kingdom of Judah in 605–586 BC by the Babylonians. In the case of Judah, it was a seventy-year captivity to rest the land for all the sabbath years that had been violated (see 2 Chronicles 36:17–21).

35. THE TIME IT DID NOT REST: By implication, because they had violated the Sabbath repeatedly. This violation became the basis of the later seventy-year Babylonian captivity (see 2 Chronicles 36:20–21).

38. PERISH AMONG THE NATIONS: The ten tribes of the northern kingdom of Israel never returned directly from captivity (see 2 Kings 17:7–23).

40–42. IF THEY CONFESS . . . I WILL REMEMBER MY COVENANT: God's covenant was rooted in the relationship He had initiated with His people. He would honor true repentance.

42. JACOB . . . ISAAC . . . ABRAHAM: The reverse chronological order of these names provides a look in retrospect as opposed to the actual historical sequence.

46. ON MOUNT SINAI: Much of the content of Leviticus came during Moses' two periods of forty days and nights on Sinai (see Exodus 24:16–32:6; 34:2–28; Leviticus 7:37, 38; 25:1; 27:34).

> **REDEMPTION:** *The Lord provides standard legislation to Moses for redeeming dedicated persons, animals, houses, and lands.*

27:2–7. CONSECRATES BY A VOW: This sets the gift apart from the rest of his household and possessions as a gift to the Lord and His service.

26. THE FIRSTBORN: The firstborn already belonged to the Lord (see Exodus 13:2), so the worshiper could not dedicate it a second time.

29. PERSON UNDER THE BAN: Like Achan in Joshua 7.

30. ALL THE TITHE OF THE LAND: This general tithe was given to the Levites (see Numbers 18:21–32). This is the only mention of tithe or ten percent in Leviticus. However, along with this offering, there were two other Old Testament tithes that totaled about twenty-three percent annually—the second tithe (see Deuteronomy 14:22) and the third tithe every three years (see Deuteronomy 14:28–29; 26:12).

UNLEASHING THE TEXT

1) What are some of the laws God stressed that His priests must follow?

_____

_____

_____

_____

_____

2) Leviticus 22 describes some offerings that are unacceptable to God. What made these particular offerings unacceptable?

_____

_____

_____

_____

3) What was the purpose of the feasts? Why did God want His people to celebrate them?

_____

_____

_____

_____

_____

4) What was God's purpose in establishing the year of jubilee? What was it intended to accomplish?

_____

_____

_____

_____

_____

_____

EXPLORING THE MEANING

The priests represented God's holiness. Leviticus contains many ordinances and regulations describing how the priests should carry out the different elements of their duties. But Leviticus 21 contains several rules regarding how the priests were to live their lives with even greater contradistinction to surrounding cultures or natural impulses than even the general congregation of Israel.

For example, we read, "They shall not take a wife who is a harlot or a defiled woman, nor shall they take a woman divorced from her husband; for the priest is holy to his God" (verse 7). Further additional regulations applied to those serving as the high priest, such as the restriction that he was not allowed to be close to dead bodies, even those of his own mother or father (see verse 11).

Once again, the goal of these regulations was holiness. The priests were to represent God before the people of Israel. Therefore, they were to be even more fastidiously concerned with holiness. Additionally, they were to avoid any connection with the pagan rituals and practices of other cultures—rites that included shaving their beards or cutting their flesh (see 21:5 and note on 19:27–28).

Israel's feasts show the importance of remembering God's faithfulness. "And the LORD spoke to Moses, saying, 'Speak to the children of Israel, and say to them: "The feasts of the LORD, which you shall proclaim to be holy convocations, these are My feasts"'" (Leviticus 23:1–2). Feasts, get-togethers, and other celebrations have been a common element of religious gatherings for thousands of years. Yet it's interesting to see the importance God placed on Israel coming together as a community several times a year to commemorate specific feasts.

The first of these celebrations was the Sabbath: "Six days shall work be done, but the seventh day is a Sabbath of solemn rest, a holy convocation" (verse 3). God was adamant that His people set aside one day each week for rest and worship. Another was the Passover and the Feast of Unleavened Bread, during which the Israelites were to remember God's miraculous provision during the Exodus from Egypt (see also Exodus 12:1–14). Another was the Day of Atonement, described in Leviticus 16. Still another was the Feast of Tabernacles, which was a week-long celebration of God's provision for Israel while they wandered in the wilderness.

The goal of these feasts and celebrations was at least partly worship, for each was an opportunity to present specific offerings and sacrifices to God. Yet another element of these feasts was the importance of remembering the past. God wanted His people to remember and celebrate His faithfulness so that the generations to come would not forget His gracious protection and provision.

Jubilee highlights God's work of redemption. Most Christians are familiar with the Sabbath—the practice of resting on the seventh day of each week. Interestingly, God's law in Leviticus also included a Sabbatical for the land itself. Every seventh year, the Israelites were forbidden from sowing crops or pruning their vineyards. The goal was to allow the ground itself to rest. The Israelites were allowed to use what grew naturally for food, but not for industry.

Beyond that, God instituted what we might call a super-Sabbath to take place every seventh sabbatical (or every forty-nine years). This was known as the year of Jubilee: "And you shall consecrate the fiftieth year, and proclaim liberty throughout all the land to all its inhabitants. It shall be a Jubilee for you; and each of you shall return to his possession, and each of you shall return to his family" (Leviticus. 25:10).

This Jubilee was a year-long celebration of universal redemption. People were released from their debts. Those in bondage were set free, including indentured servants and slaves. Any property that had been sold reverted back to its original owner—a law meant to protect those who had to sell their family land due to falling on hard times. In that sense, the year of Jubilee pointed ahead to God's gracious work of forgiving and restoring. It looked ahead to God's ultimate redeeming work, when He will make all things new again.

REFLECTING ON THE TEXT

5) Why was it important that the priests reflected God's holiness to the people?

_____

_____

_____

_____

6) What role does celebration and commemoration currently play in your church? In your family?

_____

_____

_____

_____

7) What are some of the ways that God has proven His faithfulness to you in the past?

_____

_____

_____

_____

_____

_____

8) How does the year of Jubilee point ahead to God's redeeming work?

_____

_____

_____

_____

_____

PERSONAL RESPONSE

9) What are some ways you are pursuing holiness such that even non-Christians can look at your life and see that you belong to God? In other words, what makes you different?

_____

_____

_____

_____

_____

_____

10) What practical steps can you take to continually remind yourself of God's faithfulness?

_____

_____

_____

_____

_____

THE EXODUS ROUTE

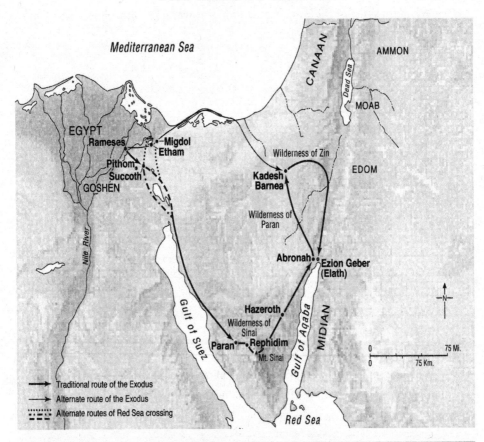

Chronology of the Exodus

Date	Event	Scripture
Fifteenth day, first month, first year	Exodus	Exod. 12
Fifteenth day, second month, first year	Arrival in Wilderness of Sin	Exod. 16:1
Third month, first year	Arrival in Wilderness of Sinai	Exod. 19:1
First day, first month, second year	Erection of Tabernacle Dedication of Altar Consecration of Levites	Exod. 40:1, 17 Num. 7:1 Num. 8:1–26
Fourteenth day, first month, second year	Passover	Num. 9:5
First day, second month, second year	Census	Num. 1:1, 18
Fourteenth day, second month, second year	Supplemental Passover	Num. 9:11
Twentieth day, second month, second year	Departure from Sinai	Num. 10:11
First month, fortieth year	In Wilderness of Zin	Num. 20:1
First day, fifth month, fortieth year	Death of Aaron	Num. 20:22–29; 33:38
First day, eleventh month, fortieth year	Moses' Address	Deut. 1:3

6

MOSES ADDRESSES GOD'S PEOPLE
Deuteronomy 1:1–2:25; 4:1–40

DRAWING NEAR

What are some of the greatest victories that you have won over the past ten years? What are some of the greatest mistakes you have made, which still stand out in your mind?

_____

_____

_____

_____

_____

THE CONTEXT

The year between 1445 and 1444 BC was a critical one for God's people. In that year, they witnessed God's power firsthand during the Exodus from Egypt and their miraculous escape from Pharaoh's army at the Red Sea. They built the tabernacle as a place of worship. They received God's law, including the Ten Commandments, at Mount Sinai. And they followed God's visible presence across the wilderness to the promised land He had reserved for them—a land flowing with milk and honey, their new home.

But, incredibly, the Israelites refused to enter this home. Despite the miracles they had witnessed God perform on their behalf, they were afraid of the Canaanites, a large and warlike people who occupied the promised land at the time (see Numbers 13:32–33). Many of God's people were so terrified by the Canaanites that they preferred a return to Egypt and its bondage (14:4). In short,

God's people rejected His redemptive plan for them. And in doing so, they rejected God Himself. As a result, God commanded the Israelites to wander as nomads in the wilderness for forty years, during which time the entire generation that had rejected God died. Under the guidance of Moses, the new generation of Israelites prepared for the moment when they would once again be presented the land promised to them—their home.

For these reasons and more, 1405 BC was another critical year for God's people. The entire congregation of the Israelites was now camped on the west side of the Jordan River, ready to cross over and officially enter Canaan for the first time. The Lord had decreed that Moses would not be accompanying them, due to his disobedience of God's commands at Meribah Kadesh, where in anger he struck the rock to bring water for the people instead of speaking to it (see Numbers 20:1–13). So, nearing his death, Moses makes a series of speeches to the people in the days and weeks before they are to take possession of the promised land. These speeches are intended to remind the Israelites of their history, to emphasize God's holy character and faithfulness, and to encourage them regarding their promised future.

KEYS TO THE TEXT

Read Deuteronomy 1:1–2:25, noting the key words and phrases indicated below.

> *A HISTORY LESSON: Moses, speaking on behalf of God, reminds*
> *the Israelites of the past mistakes they had made that had resulted*
> *in forty years of wandering in the wilderness. He also emphasizes*
> *God's continued faithfulness.*

1:1. THE WORDS WHICH MOSES SPOKE: Almost all of Deuteronomy consists of speeches Moses gave at the end of his life. According to verse 3, Moses acted on the authority of God, since his inspired words were in accordance with the commandments that God had given.

TO ALL ISRAEL: This expression is used twelve times in this book and emphasizes the unity of Israel and the universal applications of these words.

THE PLAIN OPPOSITE SUPH: Except for Jordan and the Arabah, the exact location of the places named in verse 1 is not known with certainty, although they may have been along Israel's route north from the Gulf of Aqabah (see Numbers 33). The plain referred to is the large rift valley that extends from the Sea of Galilee in the north to the Gulf of Aqabah in the south. Israel was camped east of the Jordan River in this valley.

2. ELEVEN DAYS' JOURNEY: The distance from Horeb to Kadesh Barnea was about 150 miles. Kadesh was on the southern border of the Promised Land. This trip took eleven days on foot, but for Israel it lasted thirty-eight more years.

HOREB: The usual name in Deuteronomy for Mount Sinai, meaning "desolation"—a fitting name, since the area around Sinai is barren and uninviting.

MOUNT SEIR: South of the Dead Sea in Edom.

3. THE FORTIETH YEAR: The fortieth year after the Exodus from Egypt. The years of divine judgment (see Numbers 14:33–34) were ending.

THE ELEVENTH MONTH: January–February of 1405 BC. Numbers 20–36 records the events of the fortieth year.

4. SIHON . . . OG: The two kings of the Amorites whom the Jews defeated in Transjordan (see Deuteronomy 2:24–3:11; Numbers 21:21–35).

5. ON THIS SIDE OF THE JORDAN: This verse begins Moses' first speech to the Israelites, which will conclude in Deuteronomy 4:43. Moses introduces his explanation of the law with a call to enter the land of Canaan (see 1:6–8), which had been promised by the Abrahamic Covenant from God (see Genesis 15:18–21). Throughout this book, Moses refers to that covenant promise (see, for example, Deuteronomy 1:35; 6:10, 18, 23; 11:9, 21; 26:3, 15; 31:7, 20–23; 34:4). He then gives a historical review of God's gracious acts (see 1:9–3:29) and a call to Israel for obedience to the covenant given to them by the Lord at Sinai (see 4:1–40). This introductory section ends with a brief narrative recounting the appointment of the three cities of refuge east of the Jordan River (see 4:41–43).

MOSES BEGAN TO EXPLAIN: This means to make clear, distinct, or plain. The purpose of the book of Deuteronomy was to make the sense and purpose of the law clear to the people as they entered the land. It was to be their guide to the law while living in the land. Moses did not review what happened at Horeb (Sinai), which he'd recorded in Exodus, Leviticus, and Numbers (see Exodus 20:1–Numbers 10:10), but rather gave Israel instruction in how to walk with God, and how to fulfill God's will in the land and be blessed.

7. THE LAND: The land that the Lord set before Israel to go in and possess is clearly described. "The mountains of the Amorites" refers to the hill country west of the Dead Sea. "The plain" (Arabah) is the land in the rift valley from the Sea of Galilee in the north to the Dead Sea in the south. "The mountains" are the hills that run north and south through the center of the land. These hills are to the

west of the Sea of Galilee and the Jordan River. "The lowland" refers to the low, rolling hills that sloped toward the Mediterranean coast (Shephelah). "The South" (Negev) describes the dry wasteland stretching southward from Beersheba to the wilderness. "The seacoast" refers to the land along the Mediterranean Sea. The boundaries of the land of the Canaanites were given in Numbers 34:1–15. Lebanon marked the northwestern boundary on the coast while the northeastern boundary was the Euphrates River (see Numbers 34:1–12).

8. THE LORD SWORE: God's command to take possession of this land by conquest was based on His promise of the land, given in His covenant with Abraham (see Genesis 15:18–21) and reiterated to Isaac and Jacob (see 26:3–5; 28:13–15; 35:12). These three patriarchs are mentioned seven times in Deuteronomy (1:8; 6:10; 9:5, 27; 29:13; 30:20; 34:4). The Lord sealed His promise to the patriarchs with an oath indicating that He would never change His plan (see Psalm 110:4).

10. THE STARS OF HEAVEN: The Lord had promised Abraham that his descendants would be as numerous as the stars in the sky (see Genesis 15:5; 22:17). The nation's growth proved both God's intention and ability to fulfill His original promises to Abraham.

11. A THOUSAND TIMES: A Semitic way of indicating an infinitely large number.

13. CHOOSE WISE, UNDERSTANDING, AND KNOWLEDGEABLE MEN: The fulfillment of God's promise to give Abraham such a large posterity created a problem for Moses: The nation had become too large for him to govern effectively. The solution was for Moses to appoint men to help him lead the people (see Exodus 18:13–27). These men were to be wise (men who knew how to apply their knowledge), understanding (those who had discernment and so were able to judge), and knowledgeable (experienced and respected). See Exodus 18:21.

22. LET US SEND MEN BEFORE US: When charged by Moses to take the land (see Deuteronomy 1:20–21), the people requested that spies, or scouts, be sent first. Apparently Moses took their request to the Lord, who then commanded Moses to appoint the spies (see Numbers 13:1–2). Thus, Moses selected twelve men who went to see what the land was like (see verses 17–20).

26. BUT REBELLED: Israel, at Kadesh Barnea, deliberately and defiantly refused to respond to God's command to take the land (see Numbers 14:1–9).

27. YOU COMPLAINED: Israel grumbled in their tents that the Lord hated them. They assumed that the Lord brought them from Egypt to have them destroyed by the Amorites.

28. THE ANAKIM: Literally "sons of the Anakim," the Anakites. They were early inhabitants of Canaan described as "giants" (see Deuteronomy 2:10, 21; 9:2; Numbers 13:32–33). They were larger than the Israelites and were especially feared because of their military power.

32. YOU DID NOT BELIEVE THE LORD YOUR GOD: The failure of the people to take the land at the beginning of their time in the wilderness was explained here in the same way as in Numbers 14:11. Israel did not take the Lord at His word and, therefore, did not obey His command. The Israelites' lack of obedience is explained as the outcome of their lack of faith in the Lord.

33. IN THE FIRE . . . AND IN THE CLOUD: The cloud by day and the fire by night were the means of God's direction for Israel in the wilderness (see Exodus 13:21; Numbers 9:15–23). The Lord who guided Israel through the wandering journey was the same Lord who had already searched out a place for Israel in the land. As He had directed them in the past, He would direct them also in the future.

36–38. EXCEPT CALEB . . . JOSHUA: Both Caleb and Joshua were excluded from this judgment because of their exemplary faith and obedience (see Numbers 14:24; Joshua 14:8–9).

37. THE LORD WAS ALSO ANGRY WITH ME: Although Moses' disobedience occurred almost thirty-nine years after the failure of Israel at Kadesh (see Numbers 20:1–13), he included it here with Israel's disobedience of the Lord because his disobedience was of the same kind. Moses, like Israel, failed to honor the word of the Lord and thus, in rebellion for self-glory, disobeyed God's clear command and struck the rock rather than speaking to it. Thus, he suffered the same result of God's anger and, like Israel, was not allowed to go into the land (see Numbers 20:12).

41–45. WE WILL GO UP AND FIGHT: Israel's further defiance of the Lord's command was shown by their presumption in seeking to go into the land after God said they should not. This time, they rebelled by attempting to go in and conquer the land, only to be chased back by the Amorites. The Lord showed His displeasure by not helping them or sympathizing with their defeat; for that generation, there was no escape from death in the desert during the next thirty-eight years (see Numbers 15–19).

46. YOU REMAINED IN KADESH MANY DAYS: These words suggest that the Israelites spent a large part of the thirty-eight years in the wilderness around Kadesh Barnea.

THE WILDERNESS YEARS: In this section, Moses narrates encounters with Israel's relatives: the Edomites, the Moabites, and the Ammonites.

2:1. THE WAY OF THE RED SEA: After spending a long time at Kadesh, the Israelites had set out once again at the command of the Lord through Moses. They traveled away from their promised land in a southeasterly direction from Kadesh toward the Gulf of Aqabah on the road to the Red Sea. Thus began the wanderings, that now were about to end.

SKIRTED MOUNT SEIR: Israel spent many days wandering in the vicinity of Mount Seir, the mountain range of Edom, south of the Dead Sea and extending down the eastern flank of the Arabah.

3. TURN NORTHWARD: The departure from Kadesh had been in a southeasterly direction away from the promised land, until the Lord commanded Israel to turn again northward in the direction of the promised land.

4. YOUR BRETHREN, THE DESCENDANTS OF ESAU: Esau was Jacob's brother (see Genesis 25:25–26), and his descendants, the Edomites, lived on Mount Seir. According to Numbers 20:14–21, the Edomites refused to allow Israel to pass through their land. Deuteronomy 2:8, reflecting this refusal, states that the Israelites went around the border of the descendants of Esau (that is, to the east of their territory).

5. I WILL NOT GIVE YOU ANY OF THEIR LAND: God had granted to the descendants of Esau an inheritance—Mount Seir was their possession. In verse 9, the same is said about the Moabites, and in verse 19, about the Ammonites.

8. FROM ELATH AND EZION GEBER: Two towns located just north of the Gulf of Aqabah. Israel passed to the east of Edom and to the east of Moab on their journey northward.

10. THE EMIM: Apparently a Moabite term (see verse 11) meaning "terrible ones." These people, numerous and tall, were the pre-Moabite occupants of the land of Moab.

12. THEIR POSSESSION WHICH THE LORD GAVE THEM: The Horites were Hurrians, a people who lived in various places in Syria and Canaan. Those living in the region of Seir had been displaced by the descendants of Esau, analogous to the Israelites' taking possession of their own land.

13. ZERED: A brook that ran into the Dead Sea from the southeast. It seems to have constituted the southern boundary of Moab. In contrast to the disobedience associated with Kadesh, the people obeyed the command to cross over

the brook Zered. There was a new spirit of obedience toward the Lord among the people.

14. THIRTY-EIGHT YEARS: From 1444–1406 BC. These were the years from the failure at Kadesh to the obedience at Zered. It was during this time that the rebellious generation, who had been denied access to the promised land by the oath of the Lord, had all died.

20. ZAMZUMMIM: Apparently an Ammonite term used to describe their precursors in their land. They were characterized as being as tall as the Anakim. But the Lord had destroyed them and given their land to the Ammonites. This was an encouragement to the Israelites that God could also defeat the Anakim in the land of Canaan and give that land to Israel.

23. THE AVIM: The ancient village dwellers of southwestern Palestine along the Mediterranean coast as far as the city of Gaza.

THE CAPHTORIM: Caphtor probably refers to Crete and may be a reference to an early Philistine group from that island who invaded the coast of Palestine, defeated the Avim, and then dwelt there. These Caphtorim were precursors to the later, greater Philistine invasion of c. 1200 BC.

24. RIVER ARNON: Moses continues the historical survey, detailing the defeat of two Amorite kings, Sihon and Og, and the takeover of their territory (through 3:29). The River Arnon was the northern boundary of Moab. Israel was allowed to attack Sihon the Amorite because the Amorites were not relatives of Israel.

25. FEAR OF YOU: As the conquest began, God put the fear of Israel into the hearts of their enemies.

Read Deuteronomy 4:1–40, noting the key words and phrases indicated below.

> A CALL TO OBEY: *Moses exhorts the Israelites to obey all that God has commanded—in contrast to the previous generations just described— as they prepare to take possession of the promised land.*

4:1. O ISRAEL, LISTEN: Moses calls the people to hear and obey the rules of conduct that God has given them to observe. Successful conquest and full enjoyment of life in the land would be based on submission to God's law.

THE STATUTES AND THE JUDGMENTS: The first are permanent rules for conduct fixed by the reigning authority, while the second deal with judicial decisions which served as precedents for future guidance.

2. YOU SHALL NOT ADD . . . NOR TAKE FROM: The word that God had given to Israel through Moses was complete and sufficient to direct the people. Thus, this law, the gift of God at Horeb, could not be supplemented or reduced. Anything that adulterated or contradicted God's law would not be tolerated (see 12:32; Proverbs 30:6; Revelation 22:18–19).

3–4. BAAL PEOR: Moses uses the incident at Baal Peor (see Numbers 25:1–9) to illustrate from the Israelites' own history that their very lives depended on obeying God's law. Only those who had held fast to the Lord by obeying His commands were alive that day to hear Moses.

6. BE CAREFUL TO OBSERVE: Israel's obedience to God's law would provide a testimony to the world that God was near to His people and that His laws were righteous. One purpose of the law was to make Israel morally and spiritually unique among all the nations and, therefore, draw those nations to the true and living God. They were from their beginnings to be a witness nation. Although they failed and have been temporarily set aside, the prophets revealed that in the future kingdom of Messiah, they will be a nation of faithful witnesses (see Isaiah 45:14; Zechariah 8:23).

A WISE AND UNDERSTANDING PEOPLE: Surrounding nations were to see three things in Israel: First, the Israelites would know how to apply God's knowledge so they would show discernment and the ability to judge matters accurately.

7. GOD SO NEAR TO IT: Second, faithfulness to the Lord would allow the nations to see that God had established intimacy with Israel.

8. STATUTES AND RIGHTEOUS JUDGMENTS: Finally, the nations would see that Israel's law was distinctive, for its source was the Lord, indicating that its character was righteous.

9. TAKE HEED TO YOURSELF: This section (through verse 31) carries the most basic lesson for Israel to learn—to fear and reverence God.

TEACH THEM TO YOUR CHILDREN: Deuteronomy emphasizes the responsibility of parents to pass on their experiences with God and the knowledge they have gained from Him to their children (see 6:7; 11:19).

10. ESPECIALLY CONCERNING THE DAY: One experience of Israel to be passed on from generation to generation was the great theophany (the self-revelation of God in physical form) which took place at Horeb (see Exodus 19:9–20:19).

12. NO FORM: Israel was to remember that when God revealed Himself at Sinai, His presence came through His voice—that is, the sound of His words. They did not see Him. God is Spirit (see John 4:24), which rules out any idolatrous

representation of God in any physical form (see Deuteronomy 4:16–18) or any worship of the created order (see verse 19).

13. THE TEN COMMANDMENTS: Literally "ten statements," from which comes the term *Decalogue*. These summarize and epitomize all the commandments the Lord gave to Israel through Moses. Although the phrase occurs only here, in 10:4, and in Exodus 34:28, there are twenty-six more references to it in Deuteronomy.

15–19. A strong emphasis is made on commandments one and two (see Romans 1:18–23).

20. THE IRON FURNACE: A fire was used to heat iron sufficiently to be hammered into different shapes or welded to other objects. The iron furnace here suggests that Israel's time in Egypt was a period of ordeal, testing, and purifying for the Hebrews, readying them for usefulness as God's witness nation.

24. A JEALOUS GOD: God is zealous to protect what belongs to Him; therefore, He will not allow another to have the honor that is due Him alone (see Isaiah 42:8; 48:11).

25–31. In fact, this section briefly outlines the future judgment of Israel, which culminated in the ten northern tribes being exiled to Assyria (c. 722 BC; see 2 Kings 17) and the two southern tribes being deported to Babylon (c. 605–586 BC; see 2 Kings 24–25). Although the Jews returned in the days of Ezra and Nehemiah (c. 538–445 BC), they never regained their autonomy or dominance. Thus, the days of promised restoration and return look forward to Messiah's return to set up the millennial kingdom.

27. THE LORD WILL SCATTER YOU: Moses warned Israel that the judgment for idolatry would be their dispersion among the nations by the Lord (see Deuteronomy 28:64–67).

30. THE LATTER DAYS: Literally "the end of days." Moses saw in the distant future a time when repentant Israel would turn again to the Lord and obey Him. Throughout the Pentateuch, "the latter days" refers to the time when the Messiah would establish His kingdom (see Genesis 49:1, 8–12; Numbers 24:14–24; Deuteronomy 32:39–43).

31. THE COVENANT OF YOUR FATHERS: God mercifully will ultimately fulfill the covenant He originally made with Abraham, Isaac, and Jacob with repentant Israel in the future. God will not forget the promise that He has given to Abraham and his seed (see Romans 11:25–27).

32–40. A historical apologetic, appealing for the nation's obedience to God's law.

32–39. SINCE THE DAY THAT GOD CREATED MAN ON THE EARTH: In all of human history, no other nation has had the privilege that Israel had of hearing God speak, as He did in giving the law at Mount Sinai, and surviving such an awesome experience. Nor had any other people been so blessed, chosen, and delivered from bondage by such mighty miracles as Israel saw. God did this to reveal to them that He alone is God (see verses 35, 39).

37. HIS PRESENCE: Literally "His face." God Himself had brought Israel out of Egypt. The Exodus resulted from the electing love that God had for the patriarchs and their descendants.

40. YOU SHALL THEREFORE KEEP HIS STATUTES: Such gracious privilege, as remembered in verses 32–39, should elicit obedience, particularly in view of the unconditional promise that the land will be theirs permanently ("for all time") as is detailed in Deuteronomy 29 and 30.

UNLEASHING THE TEXT

1) Why was it important for the Israelites to recall their history?

_____

_____

_____

_____

_____

2) What were the primary factors in Israel's past rebellion against God?

_____

_____

_____

_____

_____

3) How had God shown His faithfulness to the Israelites during their time in the wilderness?

_____

_____

_____

_____

_____

4)   What is idolatry? Why is it sinful?

_____

_____

_____

_____

_____

EXPLORING THE MEANING

Sin always carries consequences. The first chapter of Deuteronomy is a reminder that sin is serious and always brings with it consequences. When the Israelites first encountered the promised land, they refused to take possession of it because they were afraid of its inhabitants. Then, after the Lord proclaimed that none of them would enter the land because of their disobedience, they decided to attack the people of Canaan on their own.

First the people had rebelled against God by not taking action. Then they rebelled against God by taking action that He had not sanctioned. Not surprisingly, the attack went badly: "And the LORD said to me, 'Tell them, "Do not go up nor fight, for I am not among you; lest you be defeated before your enemies."' So I spoke to you; yet you would not listen, but rebelled against the command of the LORD, and presumptuously went up into the mountain. And the Amorites who dwelt in that mountain came out against you and chased you as bees do, and drove you back from Seir to Hormah. Then you returned and wept before the LORD, but the LORD would not listen to your voice nor give ear to you" (verses 42–45).

Moses, especially, was not exempt from the consequences of his sin either. He disobeyed God in the wilderness of Kadesh by striking a rock to produce water, thus taking some of the glory for himself rather than God (see Numbers 20:1–13). As a result, God proclaimed that Moses would not enter the promised land. Instead, "Joshua the son of Nun, who stands before you, he shall go in there. Encourage him, for he shall cause Israel to inherit it" (Deuteronomy 1:38).

One spiritual principle that is clear throughout the Bible is that sin separates people from God. Yet it is important to note that while our sin always carries consequences, forgiveness and restoration are available for the truly repentant. Moses was prevented from entering the promised land because of his disobedience—a critical consequence. However, he repented and was restored to a right relationship with God. Likewise, we will encounter consequences when we rebel against God, yet we who know and love the Lord can always turn to Him to receive forgiveness and restoration.

History is valuable. Moses could have taken many tacks in speaking these final words to the people of Israel. Yet he chose to begin with their recent history. Specifically, he began with their moment of greatest transgression and shame: "The LORD our God spoke to us in Horeb, saying: 'You have dwelt long enough at this mountain. Turn and take your journey, and go to the mountains of the Amorites . . . to the land of the Canaanites and to Lebanon, as far as the great river, the River Euphrates. See, I have set the land before you; go in and possess the land which the Lord swore to your fathers—to Abraham, Isaac, and Jacob—to give to them and their descendants after them'" (Deuteronomy 1:6–8).

Israel's refusal to obey this command was the beginning of a downward spiral that led to an entire generation perishing in the wilderness, far from the home the Lord had designed for them in Canaan. Moses wanted to burn that moment into the people's collective memory—not to punish them, but so that they would avoid repeating the same sinful pattern.

Today, it is common for us to attempt to bury our misdeeds. We don't like to think about our past sins or acknowledge the consequences we've reaped, so we do our best to pretend they never happened. This is dangerous and dishonest. True repentance means acknowledging our sin and turning from it. And in God's sovereignty, our sinful pasts equip us to encourage and strengthen others facing similar struggles. God's people are engaged in a daily battle against sin, but by His grace, we can find victory. And honestly acknowledging your past mistakes and failures can be a critical tool for moving forward in greater obedience to God's will.

Idolatry is the core of disobedience. Deuteronomy 4 begins with Moses' call for the Israelites to focus on obeying God's commands: "Now, O Israel, listen to the statutes and the judgments which I teach you to observe, that you may live, and go in and possess the land which the LORD God of your fathers is giving you" (verse 1). Following that call, Moses emphasized the importance of avoiding idolatry, especially as they entered the new situations and temptations of their new homeland: "Take careful heed to yourselves, for you saw no form when the LORD spoke to you at Horeb out of the midst of the fire, lest you act corruptly and make for yourselves a carved image in the form of any figure" (verses 15–16).

The two ideas are connected in a critical way. Namely, idolatry is at the core of our decisions to disobey God's will and walk in a direction that is contrary to His plans. What is idolatry? It is simply worshiping *anything* other than the Lord God. It is taking something that is not God and putting it in God's place. When we know what God has commanded and yet choose to disobey His will, we set ourselves in God's place, worshiping our own desires or plans, and taking on authority that belongs to Him alone. And, just as the Israelites experienced, the consequences of such idolatry are immense—because God is a jealous God, as we'll see in the next section.

REFLECTING ON THE TEXT

5) What were the consequences of Israel's rebellion against God? What consequences have you faced for rebelling against His Word?

_____

_____

_____

_____

_____

_____

6) What are some common reasons people rebel against God and reject His will?

_____

_____

_____

_____

_____

7) How does recalling God's faithfulness help you to obey and trust Him?

_____

_____

_____

_____

_____

_____

8) What kinds of idolatry dominate the world today? How do those various idols pose a threat or a temptation to you?

_____

_____

_____

_____

_____

_____

PERSONAL RESPONSE

9) Are there any areas in your life where you are currently disobeying God? If so, what will you do to address those areas and return to obedience?

_____

_____

_____

_____

_____

_____

10) What steps can you take to remember and learn from your past sins?

_____

_____

_____

_____

_____

_____

7

ISRAEL'S RELATIONSHIP WITH GOD
Deuteronomy 6:1–7:11; 8:1–11:32

DRAWING NEAR
What are some key principles that you try to live by each day?

_____

_____

_____

_____

_____

THE CONTEXT
In the previous lesson, we saw that Moses began his final addresses to the Israelites by reminding them of their history. Specifically, he reminded the people of their past decisions to disobey God and the consequences those decisions bore, including forty years of wandering in the wilderness. Moses then also warned the people about the future dangers they'd face in the land of Canaan, foremost of which was idolatry.

Moses' second address in Deuteronomy is a long one, stretching from the end of chapter 4 all the way through the end of chapter 28. In many ways, this address communicates the core message of the book. Speaking just weeks before his death, Moses gave the Israelites a clear understanding of their covenant with God. This included showing them what the law directed concerning their relationship with the Lord, in addition to the blessings or curses they would experience based on their obedience to that covenant.

In this lesson, we take a deeper look at Moses' explanation of the greatest commandment within the law and Israel's status as God's chosen people. We will also explore the ways that Moses again reminded the Israelites of their past disobedience, including his retelling of a conversation between the Lord and himself, in which he pleaded with God not to destroy His chosen people.

KEYS TO THE TEXT

Read Deuteronomy 6:1–7:11, noting the key words and phrases indicated below.

> THE GREATEST COMMANDMENT: *Moses highlights the primary command for God's people to obey: to love the Lord with all their heart, soul, and strength.*

6:1. NOW THIS IS THE COMMANDMENT: The heart of Deuteronomy is in this long second speech by Moses, which stretches from 4:44–28:68.

2. THAT YOUR DAYS MAY BE PROLONGED: Moses' concern is for successive generations to maintain the obedience to God's laws that ensures life and prosperity.

3. A LAND FLOWING WITH MILK AND HONEY: A description that includes the richness of the land that the Israelites were soon to possess (see 11:9; 26:9, 15; 27:3; 31:20).

4. HEAR, O ISRAEL: This section, known as the *Shema* (Hebrew for "hear"), has become the Jewish confession of faith, recited twice daily by the devout, along with 11:13–21 and Numbers 15:37–41. See also Mark 12:29–33.

THE LORD . . . IS ONE! The intent of these words was to give a clear statement of the truth of monotheism, that there is only one God. Thus, it has also been translated "the LORD is our God, the LORD alone." The word used for "one" in this passage does not mean "singleness," but "unity." The same word is used in Genesis 2:24, where the husband and wife were said to be "one flesh." Thus, while this verse was intended as a clear and concise statement of monotheism, it does not exclude the concept of the Trinity.

5–9. YOU SHALL LOVE THE LORD YOUR GOD: First in the list of all that was essential for the Israelites was unreserved, wholehearted commitment expressed in love to God. Since this relationship of love for God could not be represented in any material way as with idols, it had to be demonstrated in complete obedience to God's law in daily life.

6. THESE WORDS . . . IN YOUR HEART: The people were to think about these commandments and meditate on them so that obedience would not be a matter of formal legalism but a response based on understanding. The law written on the heart would be an essential characteristic of the new covenant to come (see Jeremiah 31:33).

7. TEACH THEM DILIGENTLY TO YOUR CHILDREN: The commandments were to be the subject of conversation, both inside and outside the home, from the beginning of the day to its end.

8. A SIGN ON YOUR HAND . . . FRONTLETS BETWEEN YOUR EYES: The Israelites were to continually meditate on and be directed by the commandments that God had given them. Later in Jewish history, this phrase was mistakenly taken literally, and the people tied phylacteries (boxes containing these verses) to their hands and foreheads.

WARNINGS FOR THE FUTURE: Moses now looks forward, to the day when the Israelites will occupy the promised land. He reminds them of the blessings that come through obeying God—and the curses, if they again rebel against Him.

10–11. WHEN THE LORD YOUR GOD BRINGS YOU INTO THE LAND OF WHICH HE SWORE TO YOUR FATHERS: God here reiterates that He was going to give the Israelites the land in fulfillment of the promises He had made to Abraham, Isaac, and Jacob.

13. TAKE OATHS IN HIS NAME: An oath was a solemn pledge to affirm something said as absolutely true. Invoking the Lord's name in the oath meant that a person was bound under obligation before God to fulfill that word (see Matthew 4:10; Luke 4:8).

16. MASSAH: This name actually means "testing" (see Exodus 17:1–7; Matthew 4:7; Luke 4:12).

20. WHEN YOUR SON ASKS YOU IN TIME TO COME: When a young son asked the meaning of the law, his father was to use the following pattern in explaining it to him: First, the Israelites were in bondage in Egypt (see Deuteronomy 6:21a). Second, God miraculously delivered the Israelites and judged the Egyptians (see verses 21b–22). Third, this work was in accord with His promise to the patriarchs (see verse 23). Fourth, God gave His law to Israel that His people might obey it (see verses 24–25).

25. RIGHTEOUSNESS FOR US: A true and personal relationship with God that would be manifest in the lives of the people of God. There was no place for legalism or concern about the external, since the compelling motive for this righteousness was to be love for God (see verse 5).

7:1. WHEN THE LORD YOUR GOD BRINGS YOU INTO THE LAND: This section (through verse 26) discusses how the Israelites should relate to the inhabitants of Canaan. It prescribes complete destruction for the present inhabitants, and then for the Israelites coming in to take possession God forbids intermarriage and requires the elimination of all altars and idols. It was God's time for judgment on that land.

SEVEN NATIONS: These seven peoples controlled areas of land usually centered around one or more fortified cities. Together, their population and military strength exceeded Israel's. Six of these seven are mentioned elsewhere (see Exodus 3:8); the unique nation here is the Girgashites, who are referred to in Genesis 10:16; Joshua 3:10; 24:11; and 1 Chronicles 1:14. They may have been tribal people living in northern Canaan.

2. UTTERLY DESTROY THEM: All the men, women, and children were to be put to death. Though this injunction seems extreme, the following considerations must be heeded: First, the Canaanites deserved to die for their sin (see Deuteronomy 9:4–5; see also Genesis 15:16). Second, the Canaanites persisted in their hatred of God (see Deuteronomy 7:10). Third, the Canaanites constituted a moral cancer that had the potential of introducing idolatry and immorality that would spread rapidly among the Israelites (see 20:17–18).

3. NOR SHALL YOU MAKE MARRIAGES: Because of the intimate nature of marriage, the idolatrous spouse could lead his or her mate astray. (See 1 Kings 11:1–8 for the example of Solomon.)

5. DESTROY THEIR ALTARS: This would remove any consequent temptation for the Israelites to follow the religious practices of the nations they were to displace from the land.

6. A HOLY PEOPLE TO THE LORD YOUR GOD: The basis for the command to destroy the Canaanites is found in God's election of Israel. God had set apart Israel for His own special use, and they were His treasured possession. As God's people, the Israelites needed to be separate from the moral pollution of the Canaanites.

8. THE LORD LOVES YOU ... KEEP THE OATH: God's choosing of Israel as a holy nation set apart for Himself was grounded in God's love and His faithfulness

to the promises He had made to the patriarchs, not in any merit or intrinsic goodness in Israel.

Read Deuteronomy 8:1–11:32, noting the key words and phrases indicated below.

A CAUTIONARY CONVERSATION: Moses provides a warning against forgetting the Lord and recounts a moment from forty years earlier in their history when he pleaded with God not to destroy the people after they worshiped a golden calf.

8:2. YOU SHALL REMEMBER: The people were to recall what God had done for them (see 5:15; 7:18; 8:18), and not forget (see 4:9, 23, 31; 6:12; 8:11).

TO KNOW WHAT WAS IN YOUR HEART: Israel's forty years in the wilderness was a time of God's affliction and testing so the attitude of the people toward God and His commandments could be made known. God chose to sustain His hungry people in the wilderness by a means previously unknown to them. Through this miraculous provision, God humbled the people and tested their obedience.

5. THE LORD YOUR GOD CHASTENS YOU: Israel's sojourn in the wilderness was viewed as a time of God's discipline of His children. He was seeking to correct their wayward attitude so they might be prepared to obediently go into the land.

16. TO DO YOU GOOD IN THE END: God designed the test of the wilderness so that Israel might be disciplined to obey Him. Through her obedience, she received the blessing of the land. Thus, God's design was to do good for Israel at the end of the process.

9:1. HEAR, O ISRAEL: This next part of Moses speech (through 10:11) rehearses the sins of the Israelites at Horeb (see Exodus 32).

2. THE ANAKIM: Moses remembered the people's shock when they heard the original report of the twelve spies concerning the size, strength, and number of the inhabitants of Canaan (Numbers 13:26–14:6). Therefore, he emphasizes that from a purely military and human point of view, their victory was impossible. The fear of the spies and the people focused on the Anakim, a tall, strong people who lived in the land of Canaan.

3. A CONSUMING FIRE: The Lord is pictured as a fire that burns everything in its path. So the Lord would go over into Canaan and exterminate Canaanites.

DESTROY THEM QUICKLY: Israel was to be the human agent of the Lord's destruction of the Canaanites. The military strength of the Canaanites would be destroyed quickly (see Joshua 6:1–11:23), though the complete subjugation of the land would take time (see Deuteronomy 7:22; Joshua 13:1).

4. BECAUSE OF MY RIGHTEOUSNESS: Moses emphasizes three times in Deuteronomy 9:4–6 that the victory would not be because of Israel's goodness, but entirely the work of God. It was the wickedness of the Canaanites that led to their expulsion from the land (see Romans 10:6).

6. A STIFF-NECKED PEOPLE: Literally "hard of neck," a figurative expression for the stubborn, intractable, obdurate, and unbending attitude of Israel. Moses will continue in verses 7–29 to illustrate Israel's rebellious attitude and actions toward the Lord.

7. REMEMBER!: Moses challenges Israel to call to mind the long history of their stubbornness and provocation of God, which had extended from the time of the Exodus from Egypt for forty years until the present moment on the plains of Moab.

10. THE FINGER OF GOD: God Himself had written the Ten Commandments on the two tablets of stone at Mount Sinai (see Exodus 31:18). "Finger" is used in an anthropomorphic sense.

14. BLOT OUT THEIR NAME FROM UNDER HEAVEN: God threatened to destroy the people of Israel so completely that He pictures it as an obliteration of all memory of them from the world of men. This threat was taken by Moses as an invitation to intercede for the children of Israel (see Numbers 14:11–19).

19. FOR I WAS AFRAID: See Hebrews 12:21.

20. I PRAYED FOR AARON: Moses interceded on behalf of Aaron, on whom the immediate responsibility for the Israelites' sin of the golden calf rested. Aaron had thus incurred the wrath of God, and his life was in danger (see Exodus 32:1–6). This is the only verse in the Pentateuch that specifically states that Moses prayed for Aaron.

22. TABERAH . . . MASSAH . . . KIBROTH HATTAAVAH: These three places were all associated with Israel's rebellion against the Lord. Taberah, "burning," was where the people had complained of their misfortunes (see Numbers 11:1–3). At Massah, "testing," they had found fault with everything and, in presumption, had put God to the test (see Exodus 17:1–7). At Kibroth Hattaavah, "graves of craving," the people had again incurred God's anger by complaining about their food (see Numbers 11:31–35).

23. KADESH BARNEA: There, they sinned by both lack of faith in God and disobedience (see Numbers 13–14).

24. YOU HAVE BEEN REBELLIOUS AGAINST THE LORD: Moses concluded that his dealing with Israel as God's mediator had been one of continual rebellion on Israel's part, which led to his intercession (see Deuteronomy 9:25–29).

28. THE LAND FROM WHICH YOU BROUGHT US: Moses' prayer of intercession to the Lord on behalf of Israel appealed to the Lord to forgive His people because the Egyptians could have interpreted God's destruction of Israel as His inability to fulfill His promise and as His hate for His people.

10:1–3. TWO TABLETS OF STONE LIKE THE FIRST: God had listened to Moses' intercession and dealt mercifully with the Israelites, who had broken the covenant, by rewriting the Ten Commandments on two tablets prepared for that purpose by Moses. The second tablets were made of the same material and were the same size as the first.

AN ARK OF WOOD: This refers to the Ark of the Covenant. Moses telescoped the events in these verses. Later, at the construction of the Ark of the Covenant, Moses placed the two new stone tablets within that ark (see Exodus 37:1–9).

6. MOSERAH, WHERE AARON DIED: These next verses (through verse 9) show that the priesthood of Aaron and service of the Levites were restored after the incident of the golden calf. Aaron was not killed at Sinai, but lived until the fortieth year of the Exodus, which shows the effectiveness of Moses' intercession before the Lord (see Numbers 20:22–29; 33:38–39). After Aaron's death, the priestly ministry continued in the appointment of Eleazar. Moserah is the district in which Mount Hor stands, where Aaron died (see 20:27–28; 33:38).

8. AT THAT TIME: This refers to the time that Israel was at Mount Sinai.

9. NO PORTION: The family of Levi received no real estate inheritance in the land of Canaan (see Numbers 18:20, 24).

10–11. THE LORD ALSO HEARD ME: Because of Moses' intercession, not because of their righteousness, the Israelites were camped on the banks of the Jordan River, ready to enter the promised land.

> THE CHOICE: Moses once again reminds the people that God
> has set a choice before them: Obey Him and be blessed, or reject
> Him and be punished.

12. WHAT DOES THE LORD YOUR GOD REQUIRE OF YOU?: This rhetorical question leads into Moses' statement of the five basic requirements that God expects of His people (see Micah 6:8).

TO FEAR THE LORD YOUR GOD: First, to hold God in awe and submit to Him.

TO WALK IN ALL HIS WAYS: Second, to conduct one's life in accordance with the will of God.

TO LOVE HIM: Third, to choose to set one's affections on the Lord and on Him alone.

TO SERVE THE LORD YOUR GOD: Fourth, to have the worship of God as the central focus of one's life.

13. TO KEEP THE COMMANDMENTS: Fifth, to obey the requirements the Lord had imposed.

15. THE LORD DELIGHTED ONLY IN YOUR FATHERS: God, with the same sovereignty by which He controls all things, had chosen the patriarchs and the nation of Israel to be His special people.

16. THEREFORE CIRCUMCISE . . . YOUR HEART: Moses calls the Israelites to cut away all the sin in their hearts, as the circumcision surgery cut away the skin. This would leave them with a clean relationship to God (see Deuteronomy 30:6; Leviticus 26:40–41; Jeremiah 4:4; Romans 2:29).

18. HE ADMINISTERS JUSTICE: The sovereign, authoritative God is also impartial (see Deuteronomy 10:17), as seen in His concern for the orphan, the widow, and the alien (see Leviticus 19:9–18; James 1:27).

20. TO HIM YOU SHALL HOLD FAST: The verb means "to stick to," "to cling to," or "to hold onto." As a husband is to be united to his wife (see Genesis 2:24), so Israel was to cling intimately to her God.

22. SEVENTY PERSONS: One of the great and awesome things God had done for Israel was multiplying the seventy people who went to Egypt into a nation of over two million people.

11:2. YOUR CHILDREN: Moses here distinguishes between the adults and the children in his audience. The adults were those who had seen the Exodus from Egypt as children and had experienced the Lord's discipline in the wilderness. It was to these adults that Moses could say, "Your eyes have seen every great act of the LORD which He did" (Deuteronomy 11:7). It was that specially blessed generation of adults that were called to pass on the teaching of what they had learned to their children (see verse 19).

6. DATHAN AND ABIRAM: These two sons of Eliab, of the tribe of Reuben, had rebelled against the authority of Moses, the Lord's chosen leader. The basis of their complaint was that Moses had brought Israel out of Egypt, a fertile and prosperous land, and not brought them into Canaan. Because of their rebellion

against Moses, God had judged them by having the earth open and swallow them up (see Numbers 16:12–14, 25–27, 31–33). God's judgment of their rebellion was spoken of here by Moses in the context of his contrast between the land of Egypt and the land of Canaan (see Deuteronomy 11:10–12).

10–11. THE LAND WHICH YOU GO TO POSSESS: The land of Egypt depended upon the Nile River for its fertility. By contrast, the land of Canaan depended upon the rains that came from heaven for its fertility.

WATERED IT BY FOOT: Probably a reference to carrying water to each garden or the practice of indenting the ground with foot-dug channels through which irrigating water would flow.

14. I WILL GIVE YOU THE RAIN FOR YOUR LAND: Since the land of Canaan was dependent on rainfall for its fertility, God promised, in response to Israel's obedience, to give them the rain necessary for that fertility (see verses 16–17).

THE EARLY RAIN AND THE LATTER RAIN: The early rain was the autumn rain from October to January. The latter rain was the spring rain which came through March/April.

18–21. TEACH THEM TO YOUR CHILDREN: For the children and all subsequent generations, who had not seen God's great acts "with their own eyes" as had that first generation, God's acts were to be "seen" for them in the Word of Scripture. It was to be in Moses' words that the acts of God would be put before the eyes of their children. The first priority, therefore, was given to Scripture as the means of teaching the law and grace of God.

24. EVERY PLACE . . . YOUR FOOT TREADS: In response to Israel's obedience (see verses 22–23), the Lord promised to give them all the land they personally traversed, to the extent of the boundaries that He had given. This same promise was repeated in Joshua 1:3–5. Had Israel obeyed God faithfully, her boundaries would have been enlarged to fulfill the promise made to Abraham (see Genesis 15:18). But because of Israel's disobedience, the complete promise of the whole land still remains, yet to be fulfilled in the future kingdom of Messiah (see Ezekiel 36:8–38).

29–32. BLESSING ON MOUNT GERIZIM . . . CURSE ON MOUNT EBAL: As a final motive for driving home the importance of obedience and trust in God, Moses gave instruction for a ceremony that the people were to carry out when they entered the land. They were to read the blessings and the curses of the covenant on Mount Gerizim and Mount Ebal (see Deuteronomy 27:1–14), which they actually later did (see Joshua 8:30–35).

UNLEASHING THE TEXT

1) What did God identify to His people as being the greatest commandment?

_____

_____

_____

_____

_____

_____

2) What principles were to govern the transmission of Israel's history from parents to children?

_____

_____

_____

_____

_____

3) Why were the Israelites forbidden from befriending or intermarrying with other peoples in Canaan?

_____

_____

_____

_____

_____

4) What did God mean when He said the Israelites were "stiff-necked"?

_____

_____

_____

_____

_____

_____

EXPLORING THE MEANING

God is One. Jews call it the *Shema*: "Hear, O Israel: The LORD our God, the LORD is one!" (Deuteronomy 6:4). For thousands of years, this verse has served as a central pillar for both the Jewish and Christian faiths. Today, the idea seems almost commonplace to those who have spent time in church—there is only one God. We call it monotheism.

However, when we consider this idea from the perspective of the Israelites, we can see how revolutionary it must have been. For one thing, they had endured 400 years of bondage in the land of Egypt, whose people worshiped multiple gods. That had been the Israelites' past. For another thing, since the Exodus, Israel had been traveling through polytheistic nations and territories. They had encountered (or would encounter) false gods such as Baal, Ishtar, Chemosh, Molech, and more. That was the Israelites' present.

By emphasizing such a firm declaration—"The LORD our God, the LORD is one!"—Moses wanted to make sure that the Israelites' future was founded on the truth. There is one God, and only one God. Any religion that makes a different claim is false. Any person who seeks to serve or worship anything other than God is idolatrous. That was true for Moses and the people of Israel, and it is true for us today.

Parents play a key role in the communication of truth. As mentioned earlier, Moses' addresses to the Israelites in Deuteronomy were given just weeks before his death. Moses knew his time was short, and he wanted to communicate the truth not just to the community of Israel at that moment, but also to the future generations of God's people. For that reason, Deuteronomy includes several commands and methods designed to help parents teach their children what it meant to live in covenant with God.

As Moses told the people, "These words which I command you today shall be in your heart. You shall teach them diligently to your children, and shall talk of them when you sit in your house, when you walk by the way, when you lie down, and when you rise up. You shall bind them as a sign on your hand, and they shall be as frontlets between your eyes. You shall write them on the door-posts of your house and on your gates" (6:6–9).

When you sit, when you walk, when you lie down, and when you rise. There is not much that happens during the day that isn't included in one of those four categories! Moses wanted parents to constantly speak with their children about

God's covenant. Even more, he wanted Israelite houses to include physical reminders of God's law. Later, Moses even told parents how they should respond when their children asked questions about God's laws (see verses 20–25).

Today, far too many parents have delegated the spiritual education of their children to others, even in the church. Many parents believe they are unqualified to serve as spiritual guides to their children—they believe that to be a job for pastors. That is a direct contradiction to God's Word. Now, more than ever, parents have the responsibility to disciple their children by teaching the truth, modeling the right way to serve God, and using every opportunity to help their children know, serve, and love God.

Trust and obey. Much of what Moses communicated to the Israelites in Deuteronomy can be boiled down to one central idea: Trust God. The previous generation had failed to trust God because they were terrified by the size and strength of the Canaanites. Their fear was larger than their faith.

As you read through Moses' appeals in Deuteronomy, notice that he never addressed the reality of the Canaanites. He never said, "These are the specific ways that God will help you defeat your enemies." Instead, he simply exhorted the Israelites to trust that God *would* help them: "When the LORD your God brings you into the land which you go to possess, and has cast out many nations before you, the Hittites and the Girgashites and the Amorites and the Canaanites and the Perizzites and the Hivites and the Jebusites, seven nations greater and mightier than you, and when the LORD your God delivers them over to you, you shall conquer them and utterly destroy them. You shall make no covenant with them nor show mercy to them" (7:1–2).

In short, Moses set before the current generation of Israelites the same choice that had thwarted the previous generation: Trust God or trust yourselves. In addition, he reminded the people why they *should* trust God: because of His character. "For the LORD your God is God of gods and Lord of lords, the great God, mighty and awesome, who shows no partiality nor takes a bribe. He administers justice for the fatherless and the widow, and loves the stranger, giving him food and clothing" (10:17–18). Moses added, "You shall fear the LORD your God; you shall serve Him, and to Him you shall hold fast, and take oaths in His name. He is your praise, and He is your God, who has done for you these great and awesome things which your eyes have seen" (verses 20–21). This is the God we serve today—the One who is utterly worthy of our trust.

REFLECTING ON THE TEXT

5) Why was it important for the Israelites to remember that there is just *one* God?

_____

_____

_____

_____

_____

_____

6) Who taught you the truth about God? How can you prepare now to someday teach it to your own children?

_____

_____

_____

_____

_____

_____

7) What does it look like, on a practical level, to trust God?

_____

_____

_____

_____

_____

_____

8) Do you find it easy or difficult to trust God in your current situation? Why?

_____

_____

_____

_____

_____

_____

PERSONAL RESPONSE

9) How can you prepare yourself to defend the truth that there is only one God?

_____

_____

_____

_____

_____

_____

_____

10) What specific step can you take this week to obediently live out your trust in God?

_____

_____

_____

_____

_____

_____

_____

8

LIFE IN THE NEW LAND
Deuteronomy 12:1–32; 16:1–17; 17:14–19:14; 26:1–19

DRAWING NEAR

When are some times that you had to completely destroy cherished practices or habits so that you could do the things God called you to do?

_____

_____

_____

_____

_____

_____

THE CONTEXT

In the previous lesson, we explored the opening portions of Moses' second (and longest) address to the people of Israel in the book of Deuteronomy. In those chapters, Moses repeatedly reminded the Israelites of their past sinful failures so that they could avoid them in the future. He also exhorted parents to do as he did—to continually teach their children the history of God's faithfulness so they might walk in light of it. And he showed the Israelites that they had come to a fork in the road—a moment to choose obedience and blessing or rebellion and punishment.

Many of those same themes carry through Moses' second address, which we will explore in this lesson, which also contains some new themes. For example, we will observe Moses looking to the time when Israel would fully take possession of the promised land. We will also look at the instructions he gives them for worship at the tabernacle and to regulate Israel's future kings.

Moses also prophesied about a future Prophet, whom we know as the Messiah—Jesus Christ. According to Moses, this Prophet would speak with God's voice and display the same power and authority that God displayed at Mount Horeb, when the Israelites shook with fear.

KEYS TO THE TEXT

Read Deuteronomy 12:1–32, noting the key words and phrases indicated below.

> INSTRUCTIONS FOR WORSHIP: *Moses instructs the people on what obedience looks like once they have taken possession of Canaan and God has set a site for His tabernacle.*

12:1. YOU SHALL BE CAREFUL TO OBSERVE: Moses, having delineated the general principles of Israel's relationship with the Lord in Deuteronomy 5:1–11:32, now explains (in 12:1–26:19) specific laws that will help the people subordinate every area of their lives to the Lord. These instructions were given for Israel "to observe in the land" (12:1).

2. YOU SHALL UTTERLY DESTROY: The first specific instructions that Moses gives (12:1–16:17) deal with Israel's public worship of the Lord as they come into the land. Moses begins by repeating (12:1–32) his instructions concerning what to do with the false worship centers after Israel had taken possession of the land of the Canaanites (see 7:1–6): Israel was to destroy them completely.

THE HIGH MOUNTAINS . . . THE HILLS . . . EVERY GREEN TREE: The Canaanite sanctuaries to be destroyed were located in places believed to have particular religious significance. The mountain or hill was thought to be the home of a god, and by ascending the mountain, the worshiper was in some symbolic sense closer to the deity. Certain trees were considered to be sacred and symbolized fertility, a dominant theme in Canaanite religion.

3. THEIR ALTARS . . . PILLARS . . . WOODEN IMAGES . . . CARVED IMAGES: These were elements of Canaanite worship, which included human sacrifice (see verse 31). If they remained, the people might mix the worship of God with those elements (see verse 4).

5. THE PLACE WHERE THE LORD YOUR GOD CHOOSES: Various places of worship were chosen after the people settled in Canaan, such as Mount Ebal (see

27:1–8; Joshua 8:30–35), Shechem (see Joshua 24:1–28), and Shiloh (see Joshua 18:1), which was the center of worship through the period of Judges (see Judges 21:19). The tabernacle, the Lord's dwelling place, was located in Canaan, where the Lord chose to dwell. The central importance of the tabernacle was in direct contrast to the multiple places (see Deuteronomy 12:2) where the Canaanites practiced their worship of idols. Eventually, David brought the tabernacle to Jerusalem (see 2 Samuel 6:12–19).

7. EAT . . . REJOICE: Some of the offerings were shared by the priests, Levites, and the worshipers (see Leviticus 7:15–18). The worship of God was to be holy and reverent, yet full of joy.

8. EVERY MAN DOING WHATEVER IS RIGHT IN HIS OWN EYES: There seems to have been some laxity in the offering of the sacrifices in the wilderness that was not to be allowed when the Israelites came into the promised land. This self-centered attitude became a major problem in the time of Judges (see Judges 17:6; 21:25).

15. SLAUGHTER AND EAT MEAT WITHIN ALL YOUR GATES: While sacrificial offerings were brought to the appointed centers for worship as well as the central sanctuary, the killing and eating of meat for regular eating could occur anywhere. The only restriction on eating non-sacrificial meat was the prohibition of the blood and the fat.

17–19. IN THE PLACE WHICH THE LORD YOUR GOD CHOOSES: All sacrifices and offerings had to be brought to the place chosen by God.

21. IF THE PLACE . . . IS TOO FAR: Moses envisioned the enlarging of the borders of Israel according to God's promise. This meant that people would live farther and farther away from the central sanctuary. Except for sacrificial animals, all others could be slaughtered and eaten close to home.

23. THE BLOOD IS THE LIFE: Blood represented life and was the ransom price for sins (see Genesis 9:4–6 and Leviticus 17:10–14), so blood was sacred and not to be consumed by the people. This relates to atonement (see Leviticus 16; Hebrews 9:12–14; 1 Peter 1:18–19; 1 John 1:7). By refraining from eating blood, the Israelites demonstrated respect for life and, ultimately, for the Creator of life.

29–30. TAKE HEED TO YOURSELF THAT YOU ARE NOT ENSNARED: See 2 Corinthians 6:14–7:1, where Paul gives a similar exhortation.

31. THEY BURN EVEN THEIR SONS AND DAUGHTERS: One of the detestable practices of Canaanite worship was the burning of their sons and daughters in the

fire as sacrifices to Molech (see Leviticus 18:21; 20:2–5; 1 Kings 11:7; 2 Kings 23:10; Jeremiah 32:35).

Read Deuteronomy 16:1–17, noting the key words and phrases indicated below.

> INSTRUCTIONS FOR FEASTS: *Moses reminds the people of God's command to celebrate the Passover, Feast of Weeks, and Feast of Tabernacles.*

16:1. OBSERVE: Moses discusses the feasts of Israel in this section (16:1–17), during which all the men over twenty years of age were to appear before the Lord at the central worship site. If possible, their families were to go as well (see verses 11, 14; see also Exodus 23; Leviticus 23; Numbers 28–29).

THE MONTH OF ABIB: Abib, which was later called Nisan, occurred in the spring (approximately March/April).

KEEP THE PASSOVER: The offering of Passover itself was to be only a lamb (see Exodus 12:3–11). However, additional offerings were also to be made during the Passover and the subsequent seven days of the Feast of Unleavened Bread (see 12:15–20; 13:3–10; Leviticus 23:6–8; Numbers 28:19–25). Therefore, sacrifices from both the flock and the herd were used in keeping the Passover.

3. THAT YOU MAY REMEMBER: The word "remember" was the key at Passover time, as it is for the Lord's Supper today (see Matthew 26:26–30; Luke 22:14–19; 1 Corinthians 11:23–26).

5–6. AT THE PLACE . . . GOD CHOOSES: The Passover sacrifices could no longer be killed by every family in their house (see Exodus 12:46). From this point on, the Passover sacrifices were to be killed at the central place of worship.

7. IN THE MORNING . . . GO TO YOUR TENTS: After the sacrifice of the Passover animal, the eating, and the night vigil that followed, the people would return to their lodgings or tents where they were staying for the duration of the feast.

10–12. KEEP THE FEAST OF WEEKS: Seven weeks later, Israel celebrated this second feast, also called the Feast of Harvest (see Exodus 23:16), or the day of firstfruits (see Leviticus 23:9–22; Numbers 28:26–31), and later, Pentecost (see Acts 2:1). With the grain harvest completed, this one-day festival was a time of rejoicing. The outpouring of the Holy Spirit, fifty days after the death of Christ at the Passover, was on Pentecost and gives special meaning to that day for Christians (see Joel 2:28–32; Acts 2:14–18).

13–15. OBSERVE THE FEAST OF TABERNACLES: Also called the Feast of Ingathering and the Feast of Booths (see Exodus 23:16; 34:22; Leviticus 23:33–43; Numbers 29:12–39).

Read Deuteronomy 17:14–19:14, noting the key words and phrases indicated below.

PRINCIPLES FOR KINGS, PRIESTS, AND PROPHETS: *Through Moses, God set boundaries for those who would serve Him in various leadership roles.*

17:14. A KING ... LIKE ALL THE NATIONS: In the Pentateuch, Moses anticipated the institution of the kingship (see Genesis 17:16; 35:11; 49:9–12; Numbers 24:7, 17). He foresaw the time when the people would ask for a king, and here gave explicit instruction about the qualifications of that future king.

15. FROM AMONG YOUR BRETHREN: How the Lord would make that choice was not explained, but the field was narrowed by the specification that he must be a fellow Israelite.

16–17. HE SHALL NOT MULTIPLY HORSES ... WIVES ... SILVER AND GOLD: Restrictions were placed on the king: (1) he must not acquire many horses; (2) he must not take multiple wives; and (3) he must not accumulate much silver and gold. The king was not to rely on military strength, political alliances, or wealth for his position and authority; he was to look to the Lord. David violated the last two prohibitions, while his son Solomon violated all of them. Solomon's wives brought idolatry into Jerusalem, which resulted in God's splitting the kingdom (see 1 Kings 11:1–43).

18. HE SHALL WRITE FOR HIMSELF A COPY OF THIS LAW: The ideal set forth was that of the king who was obedient to the will of God, which he learned from reading the law. The result of the king's reading the Pentateuch would be fear of the Lord and humility. The king was pictured as a scribe and scholar of Scripture. Josiah reinstituted this approach at a bleak time in Israel's history (see 2 Kings 22).

20. HIS HEART MAY NOT BE LIFTED ABOVE HIS BRETHREN: The king was not to be above God's law, any more than any other Israelite.

18:1. ALL THE TRIBE OF LEVI: Unlike the other twelve tribes, none of the tribe of Levi, including the priests, was given an allotment of land to settle and cultivate. The Levites lived in the cities assigned to them throughout the land (see Numbers 35:1–8; Joshua 21), while the priests lived near the central sanctuary, where they went to officiate in their appropriate course (see 1 Chronicles 6:57–60). Levites assisted the priests (see Numbers 3, 4, 8).

6–8. IF A LEVITE COMES FROM ANY OF YOUR GATES: If a Levite wanted to go to the central sanctuary to minister there in the Lord's name, he was permitted to do so and to receive equal support along with other Levites.

9–12. THE ABOMINATIONS OF THOSE NATIONS: Moses gives a strict injunction not to copy, imitate, or do what the polytheistic Canaanites did. Nine detestable practices of the Canaanites are delineated in these verses: (1) sacrificing children in the fire (see Deuteronomy 12:31); (2) witchcraft, seeking to determine the will of the gods by examining and interpreting omens; (3) soothsaying, attempting to control the future through power given by evil spirits; (4) interpreting omens, telling the future based on signs; (5) sorcery, inducing magical effects by drugs or some other potion; (6) conjuring spells, binding other people by magical muttering; (7) being a medium, one who supposedly communicates with the dead but actually communicates with demons; (8) being a spiritist, one who has an intimate acquaintance with the demonic, spiritual world; and (9) calling up the dead, investigating and seeking information from the dead. These evil practices were the reason the Lord was going to drive the Canaanites out of the land.

15–19. A PROPHET LIKE ME: The singular pronoun emphasizes the ultimate Prophet who was to come. Both the Old Testament (see 34:10) and the New Testament (see Acts 3:22–23; 7:37) interpret this passage as a reference to the coming Messiah, who like Moses would receive and preach divine revelation and lead His people (see John 1:21, 25, 43–45; 6:14; 7:40). In fact, Jesus was like Moses in several ways: (1) He was spared death as a baby (see Exodus 2; Matthew 2:13–23); (2) He renounced a royal court (see Philippians 2:5–8; Hebrews 11:24–27); (3) He had compassion on His people (see Numbers 27:17; Matthew 9:36); (4) He made intercession for the people (see Deuteronomy 9:18; Hebrews 7:25); (5) He spoke with God face to face (see Exodus 34:29–30; 2 Corinthians 3:7); and (6) He was the mediator of a covenant (see Deuteronomy 29:1; Hebrews 8:6–7).

20–22. WHO SPEAKS IN THE NAME OF OTHER GODS: In contrast to the true prophet, Moses predicted there would be false prophets who would come to Israel, speaking not in the name of the Lord but in the name of false gods. How could the people tell if a prophet was authentically speaking for God? Moses said, "If the thing does not happen," it was not from God. The characteristic of false prophets is the failure of their predictions always to come true. Sometimes false prophets speak and it happens as they said, but they are representing false gods and trying to turn people from the true God—they must be rejected and executed (see Deuteronomy 13:1–5). Other times, false prophets are more subtle and identify with the true God but speak lies. If ever a prophecy of such a prophet fails, he is shown to be false (see Jeremiah 28:15–17; 29:30–32).

19:1. WHEN . . . YOU DISPOSSESS THEM AND DWELL IN THEIR CITIES: The statutes that Moses explains in this part of Deuteronomy (19:1–23:14) deal broadly with social and community order. These laws focus on interpersonal relationships.

2. THREE CITIES: Three cities of refuge were to be set aside in Canaan after the conquest of the land (see Joshua 20:7 for Israel's obedience to this command). These three cities west of the Jordan River were in addition to the three already established east of the Jordan (see Deuteronomy 4:41–43 for the eastern cities of refuge).

9. ADD THREE MORE CITIES: If the Israelites had been faithful in following the Lord fully, then He would have enlarged their territory to the boundaries promised in the Abrahamic Covenant (see Genesis 15:18–21). In that case, three more cities of refuge, for a total of nine, would have been needed.

14. YOUR NEIGHBOR'S LANDMARK: These landmarks referred to stones bearing inscriptions that identified the owner of the property. Moving a neighbor's boundary stone was equivalent to stealing his property (see Proverbs 22:28; 23:10).

Read Deuteronomy 26:1–19, noting the key words and phrases indicated below.

> *REGULATIONS FOR FIRSTFRUITS: As the stipulation section of Deuteronomy comes to an end, Moses commands the people in the Lord to keep two important rituals when they had conquered the land and begun to enjoy its produce.*

26:1. IT SHALL BE, WHEN YOU COME INTO THE LAND: These two rituals include the initial firstfruits offering (see verses 1–11) and the first third-year special tithe (see verses 12–15). In both cases, there is an emphasis upon the prayer of confession to be given at the time of the rituals (see verses 5–10, 13–15). These special offerings were given in order to celebrate Israel's transition from a nomadic existence to a settled agrarian community, made possible by the Lord's blessing.

2. THE FIRST OF ALL THE PRODUCE: Baskets of the firstfruits from the first harvest Israel reaped once they were in the land of Canaan were to be taken to the tabernacle (see Exodus 23:19; 34:26; Numbers 18:12–17). This is to be distinguished from the annual Feast of Firstfruits (see Leviticus 23:9–14) celebrated in conjunction with the Passover and the Feast of Unleavened Bread.

5. YOU SHALL ANSWER AND SAY BEFORE THE LORD YOUR GOD: The offering of the firstfruits was to be accompanied by an elaborate confession of the Lord's faithfulness in preserving Israel and bringing the people into the land. The essential aspects of the worshipers' coming to the sanctuary were the presentation of the firstfruits, bowing in worship, and rejoicing in the Lord's goodness. In this manner, the visit to the sanctuary was a confession and acknowledgment of God. It was a time of praise and rejoicing because of God's goodness and mercy extended to former generations and evidence of divine sustaining grace at that time.

A SYRIAN, ABOUT TO PERISH: The word "perish" is better translated here as "wandering." The wandering Syrian was Jacob, who was every Israelite's father or ancestor. When Jacob fled from his home in Beersheba, he passed through Syria (Aram) to Mesopotamia (Aram-naharaim) to live with Laban, his uncle (see Genesis 24:10). Returning from there, Jacob was overtaken by Laban after he came through Syria at the Jabbok River, where he not only faced the wrath of Laban but also that of Esau his brother. Later, the famine in Canaan necessitated his migration to Egypt. When the Israelites became populous and powerful, they were oppressed by the Egyptians, but it was God who responded to their prayers and miraculously delivered them out of Egypt. It was God who enabled them to enter and conquer the land from which the firstfruits were presented before the altar.

12. THE TITHE: This refers to the tithe collected every third year of Israel's existence in the land of Canaan (see Deuteronomy 14:28). Apparently, this tithe was not taken to the central sanctuary, but distributed locally to Levites, immigrants, widows, and orphans.

13–14. YOU SHALL SAY BEFORE THE LORD YOUR GOD: The confession to be made in connection with the offering of this first tithe consisted of a statement of obedience (see verses 13–14) and a prayer for God's blessing (see verse 15). In this manner, the Israelites confessed their continual dependence on God and lived in obedient expectance of God's continued gracious blessing.

15. LOOK DOWN FROM . . . HEAVEN: This is the first reference to God's dwelling place being in heaven. From His abode in heaven, God had given the Israelites the land flowing with milk and honey as He had promised to the patriarchs. His continued blessing on both the people and the land was requested.

16. THIS DAY THE LORD YOUR GOD COMMANDS YOU: The last four verses of this chapter conclude Moses' explanation of the law's stipulations by calling for total commitment from Israel to the Lord and His commands. These verses can be viewed as the formal ratification of the Sinaitic Covenant between the Lord and the second generation of Israel. In accepting the terms of this agreement, acknowledging that the Lord is their God, and promising wholehearted obedience plus a desire to listen to God's voice, the Israelites were assured that they were His people and the chosen over all other nations to receive His blessings and the calling to witness to His glory to all the world (see Exodus 19:5–6).

UNLEASHING THE TEXT

1) What was God's reasoning in Deuteronomy 12 for commanding the Israelites to utterly destroy all the places when the Canaanites worshiped their gods?

_____

_____

_____

_____

_____

_____

2) Why was the Passover an important moment in Israel's history?

_____

_____

_____

_____

_____

_____

3) What commands did God give to future kings in Deuteronomy 17:14–20?

_____

_____

_____

_____

_____

4) Moses prophesied about Jesus (whom he described as "a Prophet like me") in Deuteronomy 18:15–22. What are some of the ways in which Moses prefigured Christ?

_____

_____

_____

_____

_____

EXPLORING THE MEANING

God does not tolerate idolatry. In Deuteronomy 12, Moses offered thorough instructions for how the Israelites should worship God once they took possession of the promised land. But the first was most shocking: "You shall utterly destroy all the places where the nations which you shall dispossess served their gods, on the high mountains and on the hills and under every green tree. And you shall destroy their altars, break their sacred pillars, and burn their wooden images with fire; you shall cut down the carved images of their gods and destroy their names from that place. You shall not worship the LORD your God with such things" (verses 2–4).

Ancient peoples believed that the gods inhabited specific locations—often the tops of mountains. Therefore, it was common for pagan cultures to set up sites of worship in such "high places" they connected to specific deities. Moses reminded the Israelites to have no connection to these pagan practices. He commanded Israel to utterly destroy these false places of worship. God has no tolerance for idolatry.

That is just as true today. Many believe they can worship God through means that are outside of His expressed will. For example, some try to earn God's favor by doing good works, or at least by doing more good things than bad. Others believe that holding to certain extrabiblical standards earns them righteousness, which is legalism. Others seek to incorporate rituals from other religions into their worship—including practices from different Eastern religions, such as Buddhism. Such syncretism results only in disaster because it directly violates God's command to worship nothing but Him and in no way but according to His prescription. He is Lord.

Believers can know the fullness of God through His Word. Christians today erroneously believe there is no reason to bother with God's law, since we are no longer under the Old Testament system of rituals but instead are governed by the New Testament system of grace. This is a grave mistake.

Knowing God's law is indisputably valuable because it reveals His character. Look at the instructions Moses gave to Israel's future kings in Deuteronomy 17: "Also it shall be, when he sits on the throne of his kingdom, that he shall write for himself a copy of this law in a book, from the one before the priests, the Levites. And it shall be with him, and he shall read it all the days of his life, that he may learn to fear the LORD his God and be careful to observe all the words of this law and these statutes, that his heart may not be lifted above his brethren, that he may not turn aside from the commandment to the right hand or to the left, and that he may prolong his days in his kingdom, he and his children in the midst of Israel" (verses 18–20).

God wanted Israel's kings not just to know the law, but to literally hand write a copy of that law. Not only that, but the king was required to "read it all the days of his life." Why? "That he may learn to fear the LORD." God's law communicates what God values, along with His nature and character. The more accurately and thoroughly we understand who God is, the more we will be transformed into His likeness.

Moses prophesied about the Messiah. The first five books of the Bible, recorded by Moses, contain several prophesies about the life and ministry of Jesus Christ. The first one comes in Genesis 3—the same chapter that records the fall of humanity. "So the Lord God said to the serpent . . . I will put enmity between you and the woman, and between your seed and her Seed; He shall bruise your head, and you shall bruise His heel" (verses 14–15).

The book of Deuteronomy likewise contains a famous passage about the coming Messiah. "The LORD your God will raise up for you a Prophet like me from your midst, from your brethren. Him you shall hear, according to all you desired of the LORD your God in Horeb in the day of the assembly, saying, 'Let me not hear again the voice of the LORD my God, nor let me see this great fire anymore, lest I die'" (Deuteronomy 18:15–16).

Of course, there were other prophets between Moses and Christ—men and women who spoke to the people on behalf of God. Yet there was only one Messiah whose life mirrored Moses'. Like Moses, Jesus faced death as a baby from a murderous king and was miraculously rescued. Like Moses, Jesus was the mediator of a New Covenant between God and people. Like Moses, Jesus delivered His people out of bondage.

The details of Moses' life are no accident. In God's sovereignty, His servant points us to Christ, and the fulfillment of God's redemptive plan for His people. And while our lives might not display the same overt parallels, we should likewise point people to Christ.

REFLECTING ON THE TEXT

5) In what ways does idolatry present a threat to your worship of God? How might you be tempted to compromise or capitulate when it comes to the purity of your worship?

_____

_____

_____

_____

_____

_____

_____

6) What specific and unique benefits come from knowing and studying the Old Testament?

_____

_____

_____

_____

_____

_____

_____

7) What do these passages in Deuteronomy reveal about the importance of following God's commands? What are the consequences for disobedience to God?

_____

_____

_____

_____

_____

_____

8) How might the promise of a coming Messiah have helped guard Israel from falling into old, sinful patterns?

_____

_____

_____

_____

_____

PERSONAL RESPONSE

9) Are there any ways in which your spiritual life has been influenced by legalism? What about other religious systems?

_____

_____

_____

_____

_____

10) What steps can you take to study God's law more regularly?

_____

_____

_____

_____

_____

_____

9

BLESSINGS AND CURSES

Deuteronomy 27:1–28:68

DRAWING NEAR

When was the last time you had to make a decision with major implications for your life? What was the outcome of your decision?

_____

_____

_____

_____

_____

_____

_____

_____

THE CONTEXT

Moses was in an unusual position as he spoke to the community of Israel on the plains west of the Jordan River. For forty years, he had led God's people, guiding them through the wilderness and delivering to them what God told him. For forty years, he had looked forward to the moment when Israel would finally take possession of the land God had designated for them—even though he knew it would all happen without him.

Moses was acutely aware that his time on earth was drawing to an end. The fulfillment of God's promise was rapidly approaching. Moses was speaking to a people who would live and grow without him in the decades to come. He had shared with the people about the past, but he also needed to speak of the future they would experience in the promised land.

In this lesson, we will explore the conclusion of Moses' second address to the Israelites that Deuteronomy records for us. These chapters are both simple and dramatic—in clear terms, Moses details for the people all the blessings they will receive if they remain faithful to God as they inhabit Canaan. He then also lays out the curses they will incur if they once again rebel, as their ancestors had.

KEYS TO THE TEXT

Read Deuteronomy 27:1–28:68, noting the key words and phrases indicated below.

> *DRAMATIC DECLARATIONS: Moses calls Israel to perform an elaborate ceremony to ratify their covenant with God when they enter the land. It is to remind the people how essential it is that they obey the covenant and its laws.*

27:2. WHITEWASH THEM WITH LIME: Upon the Israelites' arrival in the land of promise under Joshua, they were to erect large stone pillars. Following the method used in Egypt, they were to be prepared for writing by whitewashing with plaster. When the law was written on the stones, the white background would make it clearly visible and easily read. These inscribed stones were to offer constant testimony to all people and coming generations of their relationship to God and His law (see Deuteronomy 31:26; Joshua 24:26–27).

3. ALL THE WORDS OF THIS LAW: This is probably a reference to the entire Book of Deuteronomy.

4. MOUNT EBAL: A mountain in the center of the promised land, just to the north of the city of Shechem. It was at Shechem that the Lord first appeared to Abraham in the land, and there that Abraham built his first altar to the Lord (see Genesis 12:6–7). This mountain, where the stone pillars with the law and the altar (see Deuteronomy 27:5) were to be built, was where the curses were to be read (see verse 13).

5–7. THERE YOU SHALL BUILD AN ALTAR: In addition to setting up the stones, the Israelites were to build an altar of uncut stones. On this altar, the offerings were to be brought to the Lord, and together the people would rejoice in God's presence. This is what was done when the covenantal relationship was established at Mount

Sinai (see Exodus 24:1–8). The burnt offerings, completely consumed, represented complete devotion to God; the peace offerings expressed thanks to Him.

12–13. THESE SHALL STAND: The twelve tribes were divided into two groups of six each. The tribe of Levi was to participate in the first group. The tribes of Manasseh and Ephraim were together as the tribe of Joseph.

MOUNT GERIZIM: This was the mountain south of Mount Ebal, with the city of Shechem in the valley between, from which the blessings were to be read. Perhaps the actual arrangement provided that the priests stood by the Ark of the Covenant, in the valley between the two mountains, with six tribes located northward toward Mount Ebal and six tribes located southward toward Mount Gerizim. The priests and Levites read the curses and blessings with the people responding with the "amen" of affirmation.

TO BLESS THE PEOPLE: The blessings that were to be recited from Mount Gerizim were not recorded in this passage, no doubt omitted here to emphasize that Israel did not prove themselves obedient to the covenant and, therefore, did not enjoy the blessings.

15. CURSED IS THE ONE: Twelve offenses (listed through verse 26) serve as examples of the kind of iniquities that made one subject to the curse. These offenses might have been chosen because they are representative of sins that might escape detection and so remain secret (see verses 15, 24).

WHO MAKES A CARVED OR MOLDED IMAGE: The first curse concerned idolatry, the breaking of the first and second Commandments (see 5:7–10). To each curse all the people responded, "Amen," a word meaning "so be it." The people, thereby, indicated their understanding and agreement with the statement made.

16. TREATS HIS FATHER OR HIS MOTHER WITH CONTEMPT: To dishonor one's parents broke the fifth commandment (see 5:16).

18. MAKES THE BLIND TO WANDER: Abusing a blind man.

19. PERVERTS THE JUSTICE: Taking advantage of easily abused members of society.

20. LIES WITH HIS FATHER'S WIFE. Incest, likely with a stepmother.

21. LIES WITH ANY KIND OF ANIMAL: Bestiality (see Exodus 22:19; Leviticus 18:23; 20:15–16).

22. LIES WITH HIS SISTER: Incest with either a full or half sister.

23. LIES WITH HIS MOTHER-IN-LAW: See Leviticus 18:17; 20:14.

24. ATTACKS HIS NEIGHBOR SECRETLY: A secret attempt to murder a neighbor.

25. TAKES A BRIBE: This relates to a paid assassin.

26. DOES NOT CONFIRM ALL THE WORDS OF THIS LAW: The final curse covered all the rest of God's commandments enunciated by Moses on the plains of Moab (see Galatians 3:10). Total obedience is demanded by the law and required by God. Only the Lord Jesus Christ ever accomplished this (see 2 Corinthians 5:21).

AMEN!: All the people agreed to be obedient (see Exodus 24:1–8), a promise they would soon violate.

CURSES: *Moses clearly and succinctly describes what will happen if the Israelites obey God in Canaan—and what will happen if they do not.*

28:1–68. NOW IT SHALL COME TO PASS: In his responsibility as leader and mediator, Moses had previously told the people the promise of God's blessing and the warning that they should not turn to other gods when the covenant was given at Sinai (see Exodus 23:20–33). After their rebellion against that covenant, Moses warned them (see Leviticus 26) of the divine judgment that would come if they disobeyed. Here, Moses gives an exhortation based upon the blessings and the curses of the covenant (see Leviticus 26:1–45). The blessings and the curses in this chapter follow the same structure. First, Moses explains that the quality of Israel's future experience will come on the basis of obedience or disobedience to God (see Deuteronomy 28:1–2, 15). Second, the actual blessings and curses are stated (see verses 3–6, 16–19). Third, Moses gives a sermonic elaboration of the basic blessings and curses (see verses 7–14, 20–68). Just as the curses were given more prominence in the ceremony of 27:11–26, so the curses incurred by disobedience to the covenant were much more fully developed here. Moses' perspective is that Israel will not prove faithful to the covenant (see 31:16–18, 27), and so will not enjoy its blessings. Therefore, the curses are given much more attention.

1. IF YOU DILIGENTLY OBEY: "Diligently obey" emphasizes the need for Israel's complete obedience. The people could not legally or personally merit God's goodness and blessing, but their constant desire to obey, worship, and maintain a right relation with Him was evidence of their true faith in and love for Him (see 6:5). It was also evidence of God's gracious work in their hearts.

HIGH ABOVE ALL NATIONS: If Israel obeyed the Lord, He would give ultimate blessing in the form of preeminence above all the rest of the world (see 26:19). The indispensable condition for obtaining this blessing was salvation, resulting in obedience to the Lord, in the form of keeping His commandments. This blessing will ultimately come to pass in the millennial kingdom, particularly designed to exalt Israel's King, the Messiah, and His nation (see Zechariah 13:1–14:21; Romans 11:25–27).

3–6. BLESSED SHALL YOU BE: These beatitudes summarize the various spheres where the blessing of God would extend to Israel's life. God's favor is also intended to permeate all their endeavors as emphasized further in the expanded summary in Deuteronomy 28:7–14, on the condition of obedience (see verses 1–2, 9, 13–14). They will know victory, prosperity, purity, respect, abundance, and dominance—that is, comprehensive blessing.

6. WHEN YOU COME IN . . . GO OUT: An idiomatic way of referring to the normal, everyday activities of life (see 31:2). This is a fitting conclusion to the "blessings and curses" (verse 19), since it sums up everything.

10. CALLED BY THE NAME OF THE LORD: Israel's obedience and blessing would cause all the people of the earth to fear Israel because they were clearly the people of God. This was God's intention for them all along: to be a witness to the nations of the one true and living God and draw the Gentiles out of idol worship. They will be that witness nation in the last days (see Revelation 7:4–10; 14:1) and in the kingdom (see Zechariah 8:1–12).

13. THE HEAD AND NOT THE TAIL: Israel was to be the leader over the other nations ("the head"), not in subjection to any of them ("the tail").

15. BUT IT SHALL COME TO PASS: Moses now outlines the curses (through verse 68), as God warns His people of the price of the absence of love for Him and disobedience. (See Joshua 23:15–16.)

16–19. CURSED SHALL YOU BE: These parallel the blessings in verses 3–6.

20. UNTIL YOU ARE DESTROYED: Moses was aware that the Israelites were apt to be unfaithful to God, so he portrays in extended warnings the disastrous results of the loss of their land and their place of worship if they disobeyed God. Destruction was the ultimate calamity for Israel's sin (see verses 20–21, 24, 45, 48, 51, 61, 63).

23. BRONZE . . . IRON: The heavens would be as bright as bronze, but no rain would fall from them to water the ground. The earth would be as hard as iron, so any falling rain would run off and not penetrate (see Amos 4:7).

27. THE BOILS OF EGYPT: The disease with which God afflicted the Egyptians prior to the Exodus (see Exodus 9:9; Amos 4:10).

30. BETROTH A WIFE . . . BUILD A HOUSE . . . PLANT A VINEYARD: These three curses were in contrast to the exemptions from military service granted in

Deuteronomy 20:5–7. The exemptions were possible because God would grant His people victory in battle. Disobedience to the Lord, however, would mean that God would no longer fight for His people. Those normally exempted from military service would be forced to fight and be killed. Consequently, the soldier's betrothed wife would be violated and his house and crops taken by the foreign invader (see Jeremiah 8:10; Amos 5:11; Zephaniah 1:13).

35. BOILS WHICH CANNOT BE HEALED: Skin diseases would afflict the people cursed by God. The disease mentioned here is like that from which Job suffered (see Job 2:7).

36. THE KING WHOM YOU SET OVER YOU: Although they had no king as they entered the land, Moses anticipated that Israel would have a king over them when this curse came—a future king of Israel who would be taken with them into exile.

TO A NATION WHICH NEITHER YOU NOR YOUR FATHERS HAVE KNOWN: The Israelites would be taken captive to a nation other than Egypt, their place of recent bondage. This future nation would be particularly steeped in idolatry (see 2 Kings 17:41; Jeremiah 16:13).

49. BRING A NATION AGAINST YOU FROM AFAR: God would raise up a nation to act as His own instrument of judgment against His ungrateful people. This foreign nation is described as coming from far away, a nation that would arise quickly and completely devastate the land. This was fulfilled first by Assyria (see Isaiah 5:26; 7:18–20; 28:11; 37:18; Hosea 8:1) and then by Babylon (see Jeremiah 5:15; Lamentations 4:19; Ezekiel 17:3; Habakkuk 1:6–8).

52–57. THEY SHALL BESIEGE YOU: Ultimately, an invading nation would besiege all the cities of Judah. Moses gives a revolting description of the Israelites' response to those siege conditions. The unthinkable activity of cannibalism is introduced in Deuteronomy 28:53 and then illustrated through verse 57 (see 2 Kings 6:28–29; Lamentations 2:20; 4:10).

58. THIS GLORIOUS AND AWESOME NAME, THE LORD YOUR GOD: Israel's obedience to the law (the Sinaitic Covenant) would lead to fearing the Lord, whose name represents His presence and character. The title "LORD" (Yahweh) reveals the glory and greatness of God (see Exodus 3:15). Significantly, the phrase "the LORD your God" is used approximately 280 times in Deuteronomy.

59–60. THE LORD WILL BRING UPON YOU AND YOUR DESCENDANTS: The full measure of the divine curse would come on Israel when its disobedience had been hardened into disregard for the glorious and awesome character of God. In Deuteronomy 28:15, 45, Moses described curses for disobedience; hence, the worst of the curses come when disobedience is hardened into failure to fear God. Only God's grace would save a small remnant (see verse 62), thus keeping Israel from annihilation (see Malachi 2:2). In contrast to the promise made to Abraham in Genesis 15:5, the physical seed of Abraham under God's curse would be reduced; as God had multiplied the seed of the patriarchs in Egypt (see Exodus 1:7), He would devastate their numbers to make them as nothing until His restoration of the nation in a future day (see Deuteronomy 30:5).

61. THIS BOOK OF THE LAW: A definite, particular written document was meant, referring not just to Deuteronomy (see 31:9), but to the Pentateuch, as far as it had been written. This is evident from 28:60–61, which indicate that the diseases of Egypt were written in the book of the law, thus referring to Exodus, which records those plagues.

64. THE LORD WILL SCATTER YOU: The Jews remaining after the curses occur would be dispersed by the Lord ultimately to serve false gods, restlessly and fearfully, throughout all the nations of the earth (see Nehemiah 1:8–9; Jeremiah 30:11; Ezekiel 11:16). This dispersion began with the captivity of the northern kingdom, Israel (722 BC), then the southern kingdom, Judah (586 BC), and is still a reality today. In the future earthly kingdom of Messiah, Israel will experience its regathering in faith, salvation, and righteousness (see Isaiah 59:19–21; Jeremiah 31:31–34; Ezekiel 36:8–37:14; Zechariah 12:10–14:21). The unbearable nature of Israel's present condition was emphasized since the people longed for another time (see Deuteronomy 28:67; see also Jeremiah 44:7; Hosea 8:13; 9:3; 11:4–5).

68. BUT NO ONE WILL BUY YOU: Israel would be so abandoned by God that she would not even be able to sell herself into slavery. The curse of God would bring Israel into a seemingly hopeless condition (see Hosea 8:13; 9:3). The specific mention of Egypt could be symbolic for any lands where the Jews have been taken into bondage or sold as slaves. But it is true that after the destruction of Jerusalem in AD 70, which was a judgment on Israel's apostasy and rejection and execution of the Messiah, this prophecy was actually fulfilled. The Roman general Titus, who conquered Jerusalem and Israel, sent 17,000 adult Jews to Egypt to perform hard labor and had those under seventeen years old publicly sold. Under the Roman emperor Hadrian, countless Jews were sold and suffered such bondage and cruelty.

UNLEASHING THE TEXT

1) What purpose would the stones and the altar described in Deuteronomy 27:1–10 serve?

_____

_____

_____

_____

_____

2) What was the purpose of Moses reciting the curses to the tribes in Deuteronomy 27:11–26?

_____

_____

_____

_____

_____

3) What are some of the blessings listed in Deuteronomy 28:1–14 that the people would receive if they diligently obeyed the voice of the Lord?

_____

_____

_____

_____

_____

4) What are some of the curses listed in Deuteronomy 28:15–68 that the people would experience if they chose not to obey the Lord's word?

_____

_____

_____

_____

_____

EXPLORING THE MEANING

God's Word is worthy of honor. Deuteronomy 27 describes a powerful ceremony that God through Moses prescribed to be carried out as soon as the Israelites crossed the Jordan River and entered the promised land. "And it shall be, on the day when you cross over the Jordan to the land which the LORD your God is giving you, that you shall set up for yourselves large stones, and whitewash them with lime. You shall write on them all the words of this law, when you have crossed over, that you may enter the land which the LORD your God is giving you, 'a land flowing with milk and honey,' just as the LORD God of your fathers promised you" (verses 2–3).

After waiting more than forty years in bondage and in the wilderness, this was the *very first thing* the Israelites were to do after they reached the promised land. They were to set up huge stones, paint them white, and write on them "all the words of this law," which likely meant the entire book of Deuteronomy. Only after that was completed were the people to build an altar, make sacrifices to God, and celebrate together.

Writing God's law on those monuments would have been a huge undertaking. Not only that, but it may have seemed pointless to some Israelites. Why, then, would God make such a command? Because He knows the value of His Word. He knows the power of His Word. And He wanted His people (and, by extension, us) to know it as well.

God has always been a God of justice. In a continuation of the ceremony described above, God also commanded that representatives of Israel's twelve tribes climb two mountains within their new homeland. One group would shout blessings to those who obeyed God's commands. The other group would shout curses to the disobedient.

Several of the curses recorded in Deuteronomy 27 reflect the value God places on justice. For example, "Cursed is the one who perverts the justice due the stranger, the fatherless, and widow" (verse 19). "Cursed is the one who moves his neighbor's landmark" (verse 17). And, "Cursed is the one who takes a bribe to slay an innocent person" (verse 25).

Many other passages of Scripture reflect God's passion for justice—especially His compassion for those who have little or no ability to protect themselves. Jeremiah declared, "Thus says the LORD: 'Execute judgment and righteousness, and deliver the plundered out of the hand of the oppressor. Do no wrong and do no violence to the stranger, the fatherless, or the widow, nor shed innocent blood in this place'" (22:3). James wrote in the New Testament, "Pure and undefiled religion before God and the Father is this: to visit orphans and widows in their trouble, and to keep oneself unspotted from the world" (1:27).

There are many other examples, of course, but the theme is the same: God is a God of justice, and He has always called His people to live justly.

We are to make the same choice as the Israelites. Moses' words to the people in Deuteronomy 28 is filled with stark contrasts. The first fourteen verses describe the blessings the Israelites would receive if they remained faithful to God in their new home. For example: "Blessed shall be your basket and your kneading bowl" (verse 5), and, "The LORD will cause your enemies who rise against you to be defeated before your face; they shall come out against you one way and flee before you seven ways" (verse 7).

Then the remaining fifty-four verses describe the curses that would fall on the Israelites if they were unfaithful to God. For example, "The LORD will send on you cursing, confusion, and rebuke in all that you set your hand to do, until you are destroyed and until you perish quickly, because of the wickedness of your doings in which you have forsaken Me" (verse 20). And, "You shall carry much seed out to the field but gather little in, for the locust shall consume it. You shall plant vineyards and tend them, but you shall neither drink of the wine nor gather the grapes; for the worms shall eat them" (verses 38–39).

These blessings and curses may seem archaic to us today. However, it is critical to understand that all people in today's world have been presented with the same options. Those who obey God's Word and submit their lives accordingly will be blessed. But those who disregard the truths found in Scripture will suffer the consequences of disobedience, both in this life and for all eternity. Blessing for obedience and cursing for rebellion is a universal truth that flows from God's perfect, impartial justice.

REFLECTING ON THE TEXT

5) What are some ways to honor God's Word within the church today?

_____

_____

_____

_____

6) How do we know what justice is? What is the standard by which we determine what is just and unjust?

_____

_____

_____

_____

_____

_____

7) How does the church promote justice in the world today?

_____

_____

_____

_____

_____

_____

8) What are some of the blessings you have received for obeying God?

_____

_____

_____

_____

_____

_____

PERSONAL RESPONSE

9) How have you personally seen the importance of obeying God's Word?

_____

_____

_____

_____

_____

10) What practical steps can you take to guard your heart from rebellion (and its dire consequences)?

_____

_____

_____

_____

_____

_____

_____

10

CHANGE IN LEADERSHIP
Deuteronomy 29:1–31:29

DRAWING NEAR
Do you typically handle change well or poorly? Explain.

_____

_____

_____

_____

_____

_____

THE CONTEXT
Moses' first address to the new generation of Israelites in Deuteronomy was focused on the past. He recounted Israel's rebellion and the other transgressions that had led to their forty-year disciplining in the wilderness. Moses' second address focused on the covenant sealed between God and the Israelites at Mount Sinai. He explored in detail what it meant to live faithfully as God's people, and he repeatedly exhorted his beloved and stubborn congregation to keep the covenant when they took possession of the land God was giving them.

This section explores Moses' third address. As before, he spoke to Israel near the western shore of the Jordan River, where they were poised to cross over and officially enter the promised land. The key theme of this third address was a reaffirmation of the covenant between God and the generation of Israel entering the land. In it, Moses also looked forward to the New Covenant, which would be sealed in the future by the coming of the Messiah.

KEYS TO THE TEXT

Read Deuteronomy 29:1–31:29, noting the key words and phrases indicated below.

> *THE COVENANT RENEWED IN MOAB: Moses calls the Israelites to again affirm and commit to the covenant God had made with them.*

29:1. THESE ARE THE WORDS: The Hebrew text numbers this verse as 28:69 rather than 29:1, seeing it as the conclusion to the second address of Moses. However, as in 1:1, these words introduce what follows, serving as the introduction to Moses' third address (which runs from 29:1–30:20). In this speech, Moses provides a contrast between the covenant at Sinai and the covenant he envisioned for Israel in the future. Although the past had seen Israel's failure to keep the covenant and to trust in God, there was hope for the future. It was this hope that Moses emphasizes in the content of these chapters, focusing clearly on the themes of the New Covenant.

THE COVENANT . . . IN THE LAND OF MOAB: The majority interpretation is that the covenant in view here is the covenant made at Sinai (Horeb), now being renewed in Moab. However, this verse clearly states that the covenant of which Moses now speaks was "besides" or in addition to that previous covenant. This is *another* covenant, distinct from the one made at Sinai. Some interpreters view this other covenant as the Palestinian Covenant, which gave Israel the title to the land (see 30:5). However, the emphasis of these two chapters is not on the land, but on the change of Israel's heart (see the contrast between 29:4 and 30:6). It is exactly this change of heart that the prophets would term constituted "a new covenant" (see Jeremiah 31:31–34; Ezekiel 36:26–27). In response to Israel's certain failure under the provisions of the Sinaitic Covenant (see Deuteronomy 29:23–28), Moses anticipates the New Covenant, under which Israel would be obedient to the Lord and finally reap His blessings (see 30:1–10).

4. THE LORD HAS NOT GIVEN YOU . . . EYES TO SEE: In spite of all the people had experienced (see 29:2–3), Israel was spiritually blind to the significance of what the Lord had done for them, lacking spiritual understanding even as Moses was speaking. This spiritual blindness of Israel continues to the present day (see Romans 11:8), and it will not be reversed until Israel's future day of salvation (see verses 25–27). The Lord had not given them an understanding heart because the people had not penitently sought it (see 2 Chronicles 7:14).

9. KEEP THE WORDS OF THIS COVENANT: The spiritual experience of God's faithfulness to Israel should have led them to obey the stipulations of the Sinaitic Covenant in the future, but they could not do so without a transformed heart (see Deuteronomy 29:4, 18) and the true knowledge of God (see verse 6).

10–11. ALL OF YOU STAND TODAY BEFORE THE LORD YOUR GOD: All the people were likely stationed in an orderly way before Moses—but this is not a call to outward order, but inward devotion, to make the covenant a matter of the heart and life.

12. ENTER INTO COVENANT . . . OATH: "Enter into" expresses submission in faith and repentance before God, resulting in heart obedience. The people were to bind themselves in an oath to obey the stipulations of God's covenant (see Genesis 26:28).

14–15. NOT WITH YOU ALONE: All of Israel, present and future, were to be bound by the stipulations of the covenant to obey God and be blessed. Thus, they would be able to lead all nations to the blessedness of salvation (see John 17:20–21; Acts 2:39).

18. A ROOT BEARING BITTERNESS OR WORMWOOD: The picture is of a root spreading poison and bitterness into the whole tree. The metaphor indicates idolatry permeating Israel because of the action of an individual family or tribe, precipitating God's curse and wrath.

19. AS THOUGH THE DRUNKARD COULD BE INCLUDED WITH THE SOBER: This could be translated "to destroy the watered land along with the dry land." With either translation, the meaning is that the deceived rebel against the Lord follows only his wicked heart and cannot hide within the total community. The idolater would stand out and bear the judgment for his idolatry.

20. BLOT OUT HIS NAME: The idolater would have no place among God's people because God would curse and then kill him (see Deuteronomy 25:19; Exodus 17:14). This forceful language reveals how God feels about idolatry, which is forbidden in the Decalogue (see Exodus 20:2–7).

22. THE COMING GENERATION . . . AND THE FOREIGNER: In a future day, both Israel and the nations would see the results of God's judgment on the land of Israel because of Israel's disobedience, as a witness to the holy standard God has established in His law.

23. LIKE THE OVERTHROW OF SODOM: The Lord's future punishment of Israel was likened to that of Sodom and her allies, whom the Lord buried in fiery brimstone in the time of Abraham and Lot (see Genesis 19:24–29). Note that

Sodom and its vicinity resembled paradise, the garden of God, before its destruction (see 13:10).

29. THE SECRET THINGS . . . THOSE THINGS WHICH ARE REVEALED: God has not revealed all that could be disclosed from His infinite mind, but what He has unveiled stands sufficient for salvation, maturation in the faith, and glorifying God by obedience to His Word. God's people have always been accountable to obey only what God has revealed to them—a truth accented by the threat of divine judgment for continued sinful disobedience.

> LIFE OR DEATH: *Moses again reminds the Israelites about the blessing of returning to God.*

30:1. WHEN ALL THESE THINGS COME UPON YOU: This section (through verse 10) relates that Israel's rejection of God, and God's of Israel, and Israel's subsequent dispersion were not the end of the story of God's people. Having anticipated a time when Israel's disobedience would lead to her captivity in a foreign land, Moses looked beyond the destruction of that time of judgment to an even more distant time of restoration and redemption for Israel (see Leviticus 26:40–45). This future restoration and blessing would take place under the New Covenant.

2–3. AND YOU RETURN TO THE LORD: Moses moves to the future, when curses would be over and blessings would come. At some future time, after disobedience to the Lord brought on Israel the curses of the covenant, the people will remember that the circumstances in which they found themselves were the consequence of their disobedience and, in repentance, they will return to the Lord. This repentance will lead to a wholehearted commitment of obedience to God's commandments (see Deuteronomy 30:8) and the consequent end of Israel's distress (see verse 3). This is the ultimate salvation of Israel by faith in Christ, spoken of by Isaiah (see 54:4–8), Jeremiah (see 31:31–34; 32:37–42), Ezekiel (see 36:23–38), Hosea (see 14:1–9), Joel (see 3:16–21), Amos (see 9:11–15), Zephaniah (see 3:14–20), Zechariah (see 12:10–13:9), Malachi (3:16–4:4), and Paul (see Romans 11:25–27).

4–5. THE LORD YOUR GOD WILL GATHER YOU: The gathering of Jews out of all the countries of the earth will follow Israel's final redemption. Restoration to the land will be in fulfillment of the promise of the covenant given to Abraham (see Genesis 12:7; 13:15; 15:18–21; 17:8) and so often reiterated by Moses and the prophets.

6. THE LORD YOUR GOD WILL CIRCUMCISE YOUR HEART: This work of God in the innermost being of the individual is the true salvation that grants a new will to obey Him in place of the former spiritual insensitivity and stubbornness (see Jeremiah 9:25; Romans 2:28–29). This new heart will allow the Israelite to love the Lord wholeheartedly and is the essential feature of the New Covenant (see Deuteronomy 29:4, 18; 30:10, 17; Jeremiah 31:31–34; 32:37–42; Ezekiel 11:19; 36:26).

7. ON YOUR ENEMIES: The curses that had fallen on Israel because of disobedience will, in the future, come upon the nations that have enslaved the Jews. The judgment of God will come upon all those who cursed the physical seed of Abraham in fulfillment of Genesis 12:3.

8–9. YOU WILL AGAIN OBEY THE VOICE OF THE LORD: With a new heart under the New Covenant, Israel will obey all the commandments of the Lord. This will result in the Lord's blessing, which will bring greater prosperity than Israel has ever previously experienced.

10. TURN TO THE LORD: Here is a renewed enforcement of the indispensable fruit of salvation and another echo of the constant theme of this book.

11–12. THIS COMMANDMENT . . . IS NOT TOO MYSTERIOUS FOR YOU: After remembering the failures of the past and the prospects for the future, Moses earnestly admonishes the people to make the right choice. The issue facing them is to enjoy salvation and blessing by loving God so wholeheartedly that they will willingly live in obedience to His Word. The choice is simple, yet profound. It is stated in simple terms so they can understand and grasp what God expects of them (see Deuteronomy 30:11). Although God had spoken from heaven, He had spoken through Moses in words every person could understand (see verse 12).

13–14. NOR IS IT BEYOND THE SEA: The people did not have to search at some point beyond the sea (see verse 13). The truth was now there, through Moses, in their hearts and minds (see verse 14). All the truth necessary for choosing to love and obey God and thus avoid disobedience and cursing, they had heard and known (see verse 15). Paul quotes verses 12–14 in Romans 10:6–8.

15–18. I HAVE SET BEFORE YOU TODAY: Moses pinpoints the choice—to love and obey God is life and good, to reject God is death and evil. If the people choose to love God and obey His Word, they will enjoy all of God's blessings (see verse 16). If they refuse to love and obey Him, they will be severely punished (see verses 17–18). Paul, in speaking about salvation in the New Testaments, makes use of this appeal made by Moses (see Romans 10:1–13). Like Moses, Paul is saying that the message of salvation is plain and understandable.

19. CHOOSE LIFE: Moses forces the decision, exhorting Israel on the plains of Moab before God (heaven) and man (earth) to choose, by believing in and loving God, the life available through the New Covenant (see Deuteronomy 30:6). Sadly, Israel failed to respond to this call (see 31:16–18, 27–29). Jesus also emphasized choosing life or death. The one who believed in Him had the promise of eternal life; while the one who refused to believe faced eternal death (see John 3:1–36). Every person faces this same choice.

> A CHANGE OF LEADERSHIP: *Moses follows up his final address to the people by confirming God's choice of Joshua as his successor.*

31.1 THEN MOSES WENT AND SPOKE: Two themes dominate the last four chapters of Deuteronomy: (1) the death of Moses (31:1–2, 14, 16, 26–29; 32:48–52; 33:1; 34:1–8, 10–12) and (2) the succession of Joshua (31:1–8, 14, 23; 32:44; 34:9). These final chapters are centered around two more speeches by Moses: (1) the Song of Moses (32:1–43) and (2) the Blessings of Moses (33:1–29). Though some interpreters view 31:1 as the conclusion to the foregoing address in Deuteronomy 29–30, it is better to see these words as an introduction to what follows, based on the general pattern of Deuteronomy.

TO ALL ISRAEL: Moses addresses the words of verses 2–6 to every Israelite.

2. ONE HUNDRED AND TWENTY YEARS OLD: Moses' age at his death. According to Acts 7:30, Moses spent forty years in Midian tending sheep. Thus, the life of Moses is broken down into three forty-year periods: his first forty years were spent in Egypt (see Exodus 2:1–15), the second forty in Midian (see 2:15–4:19), and his final forty years were spent leading Israel out of Egypt and through the wilderness to the promised land. The life and ministry of Moses were completed, but God's work would go on (see Deuteronomy 31:3).

GO OUT AND COME IN: An idiom for engaging in a normal day's work and activity. Although Moses was still strong for his age (see 34:7), he admitted that he no longer could provide the daily leadership necessary for Israel. Furthermore, God would not allow him to enter the land beyond the Jordan River because of his sin at the waters of Meribah (see 32:51).

3. GOD HIMSELF CROSSES OVER . . . JOSHUA HIMSELF CROSSES OVER: Joshua was to be the new human leader over Israel (see 31:3–7, 23), but it was the Lord

Himself who was their real leader and power. He would cross over ahead of them to enable them to destroy the nations.

4. SIHON AND OG: Israel was assured that the nations of the land would be destroyed by the Lord in the same way He had recently defeated the Amorite kings, Sihon and Og, on the east side of the Jordan River (see 2:26–3:11). This was a preview of what was to come (see verse 5).

6–8. BE STRONG AND OF GOOD COURAGE: The strength and courage of the warriors of Israel would come from their confidence that their God was with them and would not forsake them. Here, Moses repeats the substance of his exhortation, this time addressing it specifically to Joshua in the presence of the people to encourage him and to remind the people that Joshua was assuming leadership with the full approval of God. This principle for faith and confidence is repeated in 31:23; Joshua 1:5–7; 2 Samuel 10:12; 2 Kings 2:2; 1 Chronicles 22:11–13; 2 Chronicles 32:1–8; and Psalm 27:14. The writer of Hebrews quotes verses 6 and 8 in Hebrews 13:5.

9. MOSES WROTE THIS LAW: At the least Moses, perhaps with the aid of some scribes or elders who assisted him in leading Israel, wrote down the law that he had explained in the first thirty-two chapters of Deuteronomy (see Deuteronomy 31:24). However, since the law explained in Deuteronomy had also been given in portions of Exodus through Numbers, it seems best to view this written law as all that is presently found in Scripture from Genesis 1 through Deuteronomy 32:47. After Moses' death, the words of Deuteronomy 32:48–34:12 were added to complete the canonical Torah, perhaps by one of the elders who had served with Moses—perhaps even Joshua.

11. YOU SHALL READ THIS LAW BEFORE ALL ISRAEL: The law that Moses wrote down was given to the priests who were required to be its custodians and protectors and to read it in the hearing of all Israel at the Feast of Tabernacles during each sabbatical year. This reading of the law every seven years was to remind the people to live in submission to their awe-inspiring God.

PREDICTION OF REBELLION: *Moses looks toward the future and expresses his fear that Israel will again sinfully rebel against God.*

14. THE TABERNACLE OF MEETING: The Lord told Moses to summon Joshua to the tent where He met Israel, and the presence of the Lord appeared in the pillar of cloud standing at the door of the Holy Place (see verse 15). This signaled

God's confirmation of Joshua, the former military captain (see Exodus 17:9–14) and spy (see Numbers 13:16), as Israel's new leader. God's message to Joshua is summed up in Deuteronomy 31:16–22.

16–21. THEY WILL FORSAKE ME AND BREAK MY COVENANT: After Moses' death, the Lord Himself tells Israel that He knows that, in spite of what He has commanded (see 30:11, 20), they will forsake Him by turning to worship other gods and, thereby, break the Sinaitic Covenant. Having forsaken God, He would then remove His blessing from them, with the inevitable result that disaster would fall on them at every turn. This is one of the saddest texts in the Old Testament. God was consistently faithful to an unfaithful people.

19. WRITE DOWN THIS SONG: The song the Lord gave Moses to teach the Israelites would be a constant reminder of their disobedience to the Lord and the results of that disobedience. The song was written that same day and is recorded in 32:1–43.

23. I WILL BE WITH YOU: Joshua was to assume his lonely role of leadership over Israel with an assurance of the companionship and strength of the Lord. God's presence with him was sufficient to enable him to meet boldly every obstacle that the future could bring (see Joshua 1:5; 3:7).

24. IN A BOOK: The words that Moses had spoken were written down in a book that was placed beside the Ark of the Covenant (see Deuteronomy 31:26). Only the Ten Commandments were placed in the ark itself (see Exodus 25:16; 31:18). The "Book of the Law" was one of the titles for the Pentateuch in the rest of Scripture (see Joshua 1:8; 8:34).

27. YOUR REBELLION AND YOUR STIFF NECK: Moses was well acquainted with Israel's obstinate ways, even in the face of the most gracious divine provision.

29. YOU WILL BECOME UTTERLY CORRUPT: Dominated by the practice of idolatry (see Deuteronomy 4:16, 25; 9:12), the people would become wicked.

EVIL WILL BEFALL YOU IN THE LATTER DAYS: The latter days (literally, "at the end of the days") referred to the far distant future. This was the time when the king would come from Judah (see Genesis 49:8–12) to defeat Israel's enemies (see Numbers 24:17–19). Here, it is revealed that it would also be a time when disaster would fall on Israel because of the evil they'd done, thus bringing the Lord's wrath. The description of God's judgment on Israel and the nations in the following song cannot be limited to the immediate future of the people as they enter the land but extends to issues which are eschatological in time and global in extent, as the song indicates (see Deuteronomy 32:1–43).

UNLEASHING THE TEXT

1) How would you describe a covenant to someone who had never heard that term?

2) What were some of the key principles in the covenant that Moses described in Deuteronomy 29?

3) What are some possible reasons why Moses kept reminding the Israelites of their choice between blessing and curse, life and death?

4) How did Moses assure the people in Deuteronomy 31 that God would be with Joshua as their new leader?

Exploring the Meaning

God always keeps His word. The text of Deuteronomy 29 begins with an intriguing sentence: "These are the words of the covenant which the Lord commanded Moses to make with the children of Israel in the land of Moab, besides the covenant which He made with them in Horeb" (verse 1). Scholars have debated exactly which covenants Moses was referencing here. Yet one fact cannot be disputed: God has chosen to enter into covenants with His people and faithfully fulfills every promise He makes.

God's first covenant was with Noah before the flood: In Genesis, God said to Noah, "Behold, I Myself am bringing floodwaters on the earth, to destroy from under heaven all flesh in which is the breath of life; everything that is on the earth shall die. But I will establish My covenant with you; and you shall go into the ark—you, your sons, your wife, and your sons' wives with you" (6:17–18). God later reaffirmed this covenant when He promised never again to flood the earth (see 8:20–9:17).

God also established a multi-part covenant with Abraham, including promising to give the land of Canaan to Abraham's descendants (see 15:1–21). This covenant God later sealed with the sign of male circumcision: "This is My covenant which you shall keep, between Me and you and your descendants after you: Every male child among you shall be circumcised" (17:10). As previously mentioned, God also established a critical covenant with the Israelites at Mount Sinai after the Exodus. And here in Deuteronomy 29-30, Moses looks ahead to the New Covenant, under which Israel would be obedient to the Lord and finally reap His blessings.

God made key promises in each of these covenants. Although His people could never keep their end of the pact, God always has been—and always will be—faithful.

Moses pointed forward to the New Covenant. Even as Moses called that generation of Israel to officially reaffirm the covenant with their God, he understood that they would not be able to uphold their part of the agreement. He knew that future generations would turn away from God, repeating the sins of the past: "You have seen all that the Lord did before your eyes in the land of Egypt . . . . Yet the Lord has not given you a heart to perceive and eyes to see and ears to hear, to this very day" (Deuteronomy 29:2, 4). In fact, God told Moses, "When I have brought them to the land flowing with milk and honey, of which I swore to their fathers, and they have eaten and filled themselves and grown fat, then they will turn to other gods and serve them; and they will provoke Me and break My covenant" (31:20).

However, in spite of Israel's coming rebellion, Moses still looked toward the future with hope. Why? He counted on the time when God would establish yet *another* covenant with His people—a New Covenant. In that day, Moses told them, "The LORD your God will circumcise your heart and the heart of your descendants, to love the LORD your God with all your heart and with all your soul, that you may live" (30:6).

Even after Israel's rebellion came to pass—resulting in their exile and the destruction of Jerusalem—the Old Testament prophets looked forward to this new covenant. Jeremiah declared, "Behold, the days are coming, says the LORD, when I will make a new covenant with the house of Israel and with the house of Judah . . . . after those days, says the LORD: I will put My law in their minds, and write it on their hearts; and I will be their God, and they shall be My people" (31:31, 33).

This new covenant included a spiritual, divine dynamic by which those who know Him would participate in the blessings of salvation. The fulfillment was to individuals, yet also to Israel as a nation (Romans 11:'16-27). In principle, this covenant begins to take effect with "a remnant according to the election of grace" (verse 5), as its spiritual aspects are realized by both Jewish and Gentile believers in the church era. It will also be realized by the people of Israel in the last days, as the streams of the Abrahamic, Davidic, and New Covenants find their confluence in the millennial kingdom ruled over by Messiah.

Training up new leaders. One of Moses' final tasks was passing the torch of leadership from himself to Joshua: "Then Moses called Joshua and said to him in the sight of all Israel, 'Be strong and of good courage, for you must go with this people to the land which the LORD has sworn to their fathers to give them, and you shall cause them to inherit it. And the LORD, He is the One who goes before you. He will be with you, He will not leave you nor forsake you; do not fear nor be dismayed'" (Deuteronomy 31:7–8).

Moses' charge from the Lord to his successor in that moment must have been powerfully inspiring for Joshua. Yet while Moses' investment in Joshua may have culminated here, it spanned the past forty years. Joshua is first mentioned as the leader of Israel's armies during their time in the wilderness, receiving military charges from Moses (see Exodus 17:9–10). Yet Moses also developed Joshua spiritually, in one of the best pictures of discipleship recorded in Scripture. When Moses ascended Mount Sinai to receive the Ten Commandments, Joshua was there (see 24:12–13). When Moses spoke with God in the tent of meeting, Joshua was there (see 33:11). And now, at the end of Moses' life, Joshua was there to take up the mantle and lead God's people into their promised land.

Discipleship has always been a key tool for spiritual development and training. Mature Christians do well to find their own Joshuas to teach and to train. And young believers can spur on their development significantly by attaching themselves to those who have been successful in cultivating a meaningful relationship with Christ.

REFLECTING ON THE TEXT

5) What can Christians learn from God's covenants with Israel?

_____

_____

_____

_____

_____

_____

6) How is the New Covenant similar to God's previous covenants? How is it different?

_____

_____

_____

_____

_____

_____

7) How have you seen discipleship done well within the church?

_____

_____

_____

_____

_____

8) What are some ways you have benefited from your relationships with older Christians?

_____

_____

_____

_____

_____

_____

PERSONAL RESPONSE

9) What responsibilities do you carry right now as a child of God? Are you fulfilling them?

_____

_____

_____

_____

_____

10) Who comes to mind as someone you can disciple? Or, who comes to mind as someone by whom you would like to be discipled?

_____

_____

_____

_____

_____

_____

11

MOSES' FINAL MOMENTS

Deuteronomy 31:30–34:12

DRAWING NEAR

What legacy or charge has been left to you by the death of someone you esteemed?

_____

_____

_____

_____

_____

_____

_____

THE CONTEXT

As we have seen in the preceding lessons, Deuteronomy is a collection of speeches Moses gave to the people of Israel as they were poised to finally enter the promised land. So far, we have studied three of those addresses; the final address differs from the others in that it was written in the form of a song—one designed to again remind the Israelites of their past, encourage them in the present, and inspire them to faithfully pursue a future filled with blessing.

The final two chapters of Deuteronomy were likely written by someone other than Moses, given that they record the events immediately before and after his death. Having led the Israelites for more than forty years—and after a total lifespan of 120 years—the Lord was ready to call His faithful servant home. These final chapters of Deuteronomy reinforce the primary themes that we have covered throughout this study. Namely, that believers in Christ today are called to repent of their sinful past and to be holy, just as God is holy.

KEYS TO THE TEXT

Read Deuteronomy 31:30–34:12, noting the key words and phrases indicated below.

> THE SONG OF MOSES: *Moses' final address to the people condenses the key concepts he'd sought to impress on their hearts and minds into a psalm for Israel to sing and remember.*

31:30. THEN MOSES SPOKE . . . THIS SONG: This prophetic, poetic song has as its central theme Israel's apostasy, which brings God's certain judgment. Ezekiel 16 should be studied as a comparison to Deuteronomy 32.

32:1. GIVE EAR, O HEAVENS . . . HEAR, O EARTH . . . RIGHTEOUS AND UPRIGHT IS HE: Moses begins the song with a short introduction emphasizing God's steadfastness and the nation's fickleness (see Deuteronomy 32:1–6). All of creation is called to be an audience to hear the message to Israel, as in 30:19, because the truth Moses was about to proclaim concerned the whole universe. It did so because it involved (1) the honor of God the Creator so disregarded by sinners, (2) the justification of God so righteous in all His ways, and (3) the manifestation in heaven and earth of God's judgment and salvation (see verse 43).

2. MY TEACHING: Moses imparts instruction that if received would, like rain, dew, raindrops, and showers to the earth, bring benefit to the hearts and the minds of the hearers.

3. ASCRIBE GREATNESS TO OUR GOD: This command refers to the greatness of God revealed in His acts of omnipotence.

4. THE ROCK: This word, representing the stability and permanence of God, is placed at the beginning of the verse for emphasis and is followed by a series of phrases that elaborate the attributes of God as the Rock of Israel—one of the principal themes in this song (see verses 15, 18, 30, 31), emphasizing the unchanging nature of God in contrast to the unfaithful nature of the people.

5. A PERVERSE AND CROOKED GENERATION: Israel, in contrast to God, was warped and twisted. Jesus used this phrase in Matthew 17:17 of an unbelieving generation, as did Paul in Philippians 2:15 of the dark world of mankind in rebellion against God.

6. IS HE NOT YOUR FATHER, WHO BOUGHT YOU: Israel's foolishness and stupidity would be evident in the fact that they would rebel against God, who as a Father had brought them forth and formed them into a nation. As Father, He was the progenitor and originator of the nation and the One who had matured and sustained it. This idea of God as Father of the nation is emphasized in the Old Testament (see 1 Chronicles 29:10; Isaiah 63:16; 64:8; Malachi 2:10), while the idea of God as Father of individual believers is developed in the New Testament (see Romans 8:15; Galatians 4:6).

7. REMEMBER THE DAYS OF OLD: A call to reflect on past history and to inquire about the lessons to be learned.

8–9. THE MOST HIGH: This title for God emphasizes His sovereignty and authority over all the nations (see Genesis 11:9; 10:32; 14:18; Numbers 24:16) with the amazing revelation that, in the plan for the world, God determined to save His chosen people. God ordained a plan where the number of nations (seventy, according to Genesis 10) corresponded to the number of the children of Jacob, who was Israel (seventy, according to Genesis 46:27). Further, as God gave the nations their lands, He established their boundaries, leaving Israel enough land to sustain their expected population.

10. HE FOUND HIM IN A DESERT LAND: This description (through verse 14) of what God did for Israel is figurative. Israel is likened to a man in the harsh desert in danger of death, without food or water, whom the Lord rescues.

AS THE APPLE OF HIS EYE: The pupil. Just as the pupil of the eye is essential for vision and, therefore, closely protected—especially in a howling wind—so God closely protected Israel (see Psalm 17:8; Proverbs 7:2).

11. AS AN EAGLE ... HOVERS OVER ITS YOUNG: Moses describes the Lord's care for Israel from the time of the wilderness wanderings (see Deuteronomy 32:11–12) to their possession and initial enjoyment of the blessings of the land (see verses 13–14). The Lord has exercised His loving care for Israel like an eagle caring for its young, particularly as fledglings. As eaglets begin to fly but have little strength, they start to fall. At that point, a parent eagle will stop the fledgling's fall by spreading its wings so the baby can land on them. In the same way, the Lord has carried Israel and not let the nation fall. He had been training Israel to depend on His love and omnipotence.

12. NO FOREIGN GOD: Moses makes clear that God alone carried Israel through all its struggles and victories, thus depriving the people of any excuse for apostasy from the Lord by interest in false gods.

13. HE MADE HIM DRAW HONEY FROM THE ROCK: This reference to honey-combs, located in the fissures of the faces of a cliff, is used because Canaan had many wild bees.

OIL FROM THE FLINTY ROCK: This is likely a reference to olive trees growing in rocky places, otherwise bereft of fruit-growing trees. These metaphoric phrases regarding honey and oil point to the most valuable products coming out of the most unproductive places.

15. JESHURUN: The word means "righteous" (literally, "the upright one"), a name for Israel that sarcastically expresses the fact that Israel will not live up to God's law after entering the land. God uses this name to remind Israel of His calling and to severely rebuke their apostasy.

GREW FAT AND KICKED: Like an ox which has become fat and intractable, Israel will become affluent because of the bountiful provisions of God, but in-stead of being thankful and obedient, she will grow rebellious against the Lord (see 6:10–15). Israel's apostasy (see 32:15–18) would bring about God's future outpouring of wrath on His people (see 32:19–27) and Israel's continuing blind-ness in the face of God's wrath (see verses 28–33).

16. FOREIGN GODS: Israel will turn to worship the gods of the people in the land. These were gods they had not before acknowledged (see verse 17).

17. DEMONS: See Leviticus 17:7, 2 Chronicles 11:15, and Psalm 106:37. The term describes those angels who fell with Satan and constitute the evil force that fights against God and His holy angels. Idol worship is a form of demon worship, as demon spirits impersonate the idol and work their wicked strategies through the system of false religion tied to the false god.

19–33. AND WHEN THE LORD SAW IT, HE SPURNED THEM: In this section of Moses' song, he describes how the Lord will severely judge Israel for her fool-ish apostasy but how Israel will continue in blindness (verses 19–27) even in the face of that wrath (verses 28–33). This visitation of anger is in the form of a divine resolution to punish the Israelites, including the next generation of sons and daughters (see verse 19), whenever they pursue idols. In verses 20–22, Moses quotes the Lord directly.

21. NOT A NATION: As the Lord would be provoked to jealousy by Israel's wor-ship of that which was "not God," so He would provoke Israel to jealousy and anger by humiliation before a foolish, vile "no-nation." In Romans 10:19, Paul applied the term "not a nation" to the Gentile nations generally. Jews who wor-ship a "no-god" will be judged by a "no-people."

22. A FIRE IS KINDLED . . . TO THE LOWEST HELL: Once the fire of God's anger is kindled, it knows no limits in its destructive force, reaching even to those in the grave, an indication of God's eternal judgment against those who oppose Him.

23–24. I WILL HEAP DISASTERS ON THEM: The disasters (literally "evil") are described in verse 24. The arrows represent the enemies who would defeat Israel in war and are further described in Deuteronomy 32:25–27.

27. OUR HAND IS HIGH: This speaks of military arrogance. The only thing that would prevent the Lord from permitting the complete destruction of His people would be His concern that the Gentiles might claim for themselves the honor of victory over Israel.

31. THEIR ROCK IS NOT LIKE OUR ROCK: A contrast between the gods of the nations ("rock") and Israel's true God ("Rock"). Israel could smite its foes with little difficulty because of the weakness of their gods, who are not like the Rock Jehovah.

32. THE VINE OF SODOM: Employing the metaphor of a vineyard, its grapes, and its wine, the wickedness of Israel's enemies was described as having its roots in Sodom and Gomorrah, the evil cities destroyed by God (see Genesis 19:1–29).

34. SEALED UP AMONG MY TREASURES: The wicked acts of Israel's enemies were known to God and are stored up in His storehouse. At the proper time, God will avenge. (Paul uses this image in Romans 2:4–5.) Ultimately, this vengeance of God would strip Israel of all power and turn the nation from idolatry (see Deuteronomy 32:34–38). Then God would bring His judgment upon the nations, both His enemies and Israel's (see verses 39–42).

35. VENGEANCE IS MINE, AND RECOMPENSE: The manner and timing of the repayment of man's wickedness is God's prerogative. This principle is reaffirmed in the New Testament in Romans 12:19 and Hebrews 10:30.

36. THE LORD WILL JUDGE HIS PEOPLE: This is the promise that the Lord will judge Israel as a nation, but that the nation is composed of righteous and wicked. God actually helps the righteous by destroying the wicked. "His servants" are the righteous, all who in the time of judgment are faithful to the Lord (see Malachi 3:16–4:3). The Lord will judge Israel, not to destroy the nation, but to punish the sinners and show the folly and impotence of their false gods (see Deuteronomy 32:37–38). At the same time, the Lord has always shown compassion for those who have loved and obeyed Him.

39. I, EVEN I, AM HE: After showing the worthlessness of false gods in verses 37–38, this declaration of the nature of God is presented in contrast to show that

the God of Israel is the living God, the only One who can offer help and protection to Israel. He has the power of life and death with regard to Israel (see 1 Samuel 2:6; 2 Kings 5:7) and the power to wound and heal them (see Isaiah 30:26; 57:17–18; Jeremiah 17:14; Hosea 6:1).

40–42. I RAISE MY HAND: God takes an oath to bring vengeance on His enemies. Here (as in Exodus 6:8; Numbers 14:28), the hand is used anthropomorphically of God, who can swear by no greater than His eternal Self (see Isaiah 45:23; Jeremiah 22:5; Hebrews 6:17).

43. REJOICE, O GENTILES, WITH HIS PEOPLE: Moses' song ends with a call to the nations to rejoice with Israel because God would punish His enemies and spiritually heal both Israel and her land. This atonement for the land is the satisfaction of God's wrath by the sacrifice of His enemies in judgment. The atonement for the people is by the sacrifice of Jesus Christ on the Cross (see Psalm 79:9). Paul quotes this passage in Romans 15:10, as does the writer of Hebrews (see 1:6).

47. IT IS YOUR LIFE: Moses reiterates to Israel that obedience to the Lord's commands is to be the key to her living long in the land that God has prepared. So he calls for this song to be a kind of national anthem, which the leaders were to see was frequently repeated in order to animate the people to obey God.

> FINAL BLESSING ON ISRAEL: *Moses offers a blessing to each of Israel's tribes.*

48. THAT VERY SAME DAY: The anticipation (see Deuteronomy 32:48–52) and subsequent record (34:1–12) of Moses' death bracket the recording of his final blessing to Israel. This literary unit, which stretches from 32:48–34:12, was composed and added to the text after the death of Moses.

49. MOUNT NEBO: A peak in the Abarim range of mountains to the east of the north end of the Dead Sea, from which Moses would be able to see across to the promised land, which God did not permit Him to enter.

50. GATHERED TO YOUR PEOPLE: An idiom for death (see Genesis 25:8, 17; 35:29; 49:33; Numbers 20:24, 26; 31:2).

33:1. THE BLESSING: The final words of Moses in this chapter are a listing of the blessings for each of the tribes of Israel, Simeon excluded (see Deuteronomy 33:6–25). These blessings were introduced and concluded with passages which praise God (see verses 2–5, 26–29). That these blessings of Moses are presented in this chapter as recorded by someone other than Moses is clear because in verse

1, Moses is viewed as already being dead, and as the words of Moses are presented, the clause "he said" is used (see verses 2, 7, 8, 12, 13, 18, 20, 22, 23, 24).

THE MAN OF GOD: This is the first use of this phrase in Scripture. Subsequently, some seventy times in the Old Testament, messengers of God (especially prophets) are called "a man of God" (see 1 Samuel 2:27; 9:6; 1 Kings 13:1; 17:18; 2 Kings 4:7). The New Testament uses this title for Timothy (see 1 Timothy 6:11; 2 Timothy 3:17). Moses is viewed among such prophets in this conclusion to the book (see Deuteronomy 34:10).

2. SINAI . . . SEIR . . . PARAN: Mountains associated with the giving of the law—Sinai on the south, Seir on the northeast, and Paran on the north. These mountains provide a beautiful metaphor, borrowed from the dawn. God, like the morning sun, is the Light that rises to give His beams to all the Promised Land.

SAINTS: Literally "holy ones." Probably a reference to the angels who assisted God when the law was mediated to Moses at Mount Sinai (see Acts 7:53; Galatians 3:19; Hebrews 2:2).

3. HE LOVES THE PEOPLE: Notwithstanding the awe-inspiring symbols of majesty displayed at Sinai, the law was given in kindness and love to provide both temporal and eternal blessing to those with a heart to obey it (see Romans 13:8–10).

5. KING IN JESHURUN: It is possible that this refers back to Moses in verse 4. However, it is more likely speaking of God since: 1) Moses is never called "king" elsewhere in Scripture; 2) Moses was not anointed to be king as were the other human kings of Israel; 3) Israel forsook God as their king when they chose Saul to be king (1 Samuel 8:7); and 4) God is elsewhere actually declared to be king over Jeshurun (Isaiah 44:1-6).

6. REUBEN: Here is the prayer that this tribe would survive in large numbers (see Numbers 1:21; 2:11).

7. JUDAH: Moses prays that this tribe would be powerful in leading the nation to be victorious in battle through the help of the Lord.

8–11. LEVI: Moses prays for the Levites to fulfill their tasks, God granting them protection from their enemies. Moses omitted Simeon, but that tribe did receive a number of allies in the southern territory of Judah (see Joshua 19:2–9) and did not lose their identity (see 1 Chronicles 4:24–38).

12. BENJAMIN: That this tribe would have security and peace because the Lord would shield them was Moses' request. They were given the land in northern Judah near Jerusalem.

13–17. JOSEPH: Including both Ephraim and Manasseh (see Deuteronomy 33:17), who would enjoy material prosperity (see verses 13–16) and military might (see verse 17), which would compensate and reward them for the Egyptian slavery of their ancestor (see Genesis 49:26). Ephraim would have greater military success in the future than Manasseh, as the outworking of Jacob's blessing of the younger over the older (see Genesis 48:20).

18. ZEBULUN . . . ISSACHAR: Moses prayed that these two tribes, from Leah's fifth and sixth sons, would receive God's blessing in their daily lives, particularly through sea trade.

20. GAD: This tribe had large territory east of the Jordan River and would be a leader in gaining the victory in battles in Canaan.

22. DAN: Dan had the potential for great energy and strength and would later leap from its southern settlement to establish a colony in the north. (See Genesis 49:17–18, where Dan is compared to a serpent).

23. NAPHTALI: This tribe would enjoy the favor of God in the fullness of His blessing, having land in the west of Galilee and south of the northern Danites.

24. ASHER: The request is that this tribe would experience abundant fertility and prosperity, depicted by reference to a foot-operated oil press. Shoes of hard metal suited both country people and soldiers.

26–27. THE GOD OF JESHURUN: Moses concludes his blessings with a reminder of the uniqueness of Israel's God.

28–29. ISRAEL SHALL DWELL IN SAFETY: This pledge was only partially fulfilled after the people entered the land, but it awaits a complete fulfillment in the kingdom of Messiah.

FOUNTAIN OF JACOB: A euphemism for Jacob's seed, referring to his posterity.

THE END OF MOSES' DAYS: The final chapter in Deuteronomy records the last days of Moses' life on earth and the enormity of his legacy.

34:1. MOSES WENT UP: This concluding chapter was obviously written by someone other than Moses (probably the writer of Joshua) to bridge from Deuteronomy to Joshua.

PISGAH: The range or ridge of which Mount Nebo was the highest point.

THE LORD SHOWED HIM: From the top of the mountain, Moses was allowed to see the panorama of the land (Canaan) the Lord had promised to give to the patriarchs and their seed in Genesis 12:7; 13:15; 15:18–21; 26:4; 28:13–14.

6. HE BURIED HIM: The context indicates that the Lord is the One who buried Moses, and no man had part in it. (See Jude 9, which recounts Michael's dispute with Satan over Moses' body.)

7. EYES WERE NOT DIM NOR HIS NATURAL VIGOR DIMINISHED: Moses' physical vision and health were not impaired. It was not death by natural causes that kept Moses from leading Israel into the promised land; it was his unfaithfulness to the Lord at Meribah (see Numbers 20:12).

8. THIRTY DAYS: The mourning period for Moses conformed to that of Aaron (see Numbers 20:29).

9. SPIRIT OF WISDOM . . . LAID HIS HANDS: Joshua received confirmation of the military and administrative ability necessary to the task the Lord had given him, as well as the spiritual wisdom to rely on and be committed to the Lord through the laying on of Moses' hands.

10. A PROPHET LIKE MOSES: Moses was the greatest of all the Old Testament prophets, one whom the Lord knew intimately. Not until John the Baptist was there another prophet greater than Moses (see Matthew 11:11). After John, the Prophet came of whom Moses wrote (see John 1:21, 25; 6:14 and compare with Deuteronomy 18:15, 18; Acts 3:22; 7:37). Moses next appeared on the Mount of Transfiguration together with Elijah and Jesus Christ (see Matthew 17:3; Mark 9:4; Luke 9:30–31).

UNLEASHING THE TEXT

1) How does reflecting on your sinful failures help you understand and appreciate God's holiness and faithfulness?

_____

_____

_____

_____

2) Which of the key themes from Leviticus and Deuteronomy are present in Moses' song in Deuteronomy 32?

_____

_____

_____

_____

_____

3) What key themes are present throughout Moses' blessings over Israel in Deuteronomy 33?

_____

_____

_____

_____

_____

_____

4) How is Moses' death described in Deuteronomy 34? What do the closing words of the book say about the legacy Moses left behind to the people of Israel?

_____

_____

_____

_____

_____

_____

_____

EXPLORING THE MEANING

God is always faithful. Moses began the book of Deuteronomy by detailing the failure of Israel's past generations when they rebelled against God in refusing to obey Him by entering the promised land. Moses ended his contribution to Deuteronomy with a song that highlights that same theme. It is important to note that in both cases, Moses also pointedly called the Israelites' attention to God's contrasting faithfulness.

"He is the Rock, His work is perfect," Moses wrote, "for all His ways are justice, a God of truth and without injustice; righteous and upright is He" (32:4). Later, Moses encouraged his hearers to remember how God had selected Israel's forefathers and lifted them up: "He found him in a desert land and in the wasteland, a howling wilderness; He encircled him, He instructed him, He kept him as the apple of His eye. As an eagle stirs up its nest, hovers over its young, spreading out its wings, taking them up, carrying them on its wings, so the LORD alone led him, and there was no foreign god with him" (verses 10–12).

Despite Israel's many and repeated transgressions, God was faithful to them in all respects. He reached out to them, nourished them, and gave them opportunity after opportunity to repent and return to a right relationship with Him. He has always been, and will always be, faithful to His chosen ones.

God alone is God. Another key theme throughout Moses' song is God's transcendent superiority, evident through comparing any other deity to Him. By God's revelation, Moses prophesied a time when Israel would worship the false gods of the surrounding nations, but Moses wanted God's people to know that they would not be trading the true God for other gods at all, but rather evil spirits: "They provoked Him to jealousy with foreign gods; with abominations they provoked Him to anger. They sacrificed to demons, not to God, to gods they did not know, to new gods, new arrivals that your fathers did not fear" (Deuteronomy 32:16–17).

So Moses concluded this final address to God's wayward people by declaring one more time to them the Lord's unmatched superiority in His own words:

> Now see that I, even I, am He,
> And there is no God besides Me;
> I kill and I make alive;
> I wound and I heal;
> Nor is there any who can deliver from My hand.
> For I raise My hand to heaven,
> And say, "As I live forever,
> If I whet My glittering sword,
> And My hand takes hold on judgment,
> I will render vengeance to My enemies,
> And repay those who hate Me (verses 39–41).

No matter what happens in the world at large, or in your world specifically, you as a Christian can trust that God is in control. He is sovereign. He is capable. And He alone is God.

Death is a reality for all people. Aside from Jesus Christ, there is no person written about in Scripture who accomplished or witnessed more than Moses. As God's prophet and a vessel for His power, Moses performed miracles on an unprecedented scale—including ushering in the ten plagues during the Exodus and leading the Israelites' escape through the Red Sea. Moses had a deep and intimate relationship with God. In fact, we read that "the LORD spoke to Moses face to face, as a man speaks to his friend" (Exodus 33:11). Despite these incredible qualifications, Scripture describes Moses as "very humble, more than all men who were on the face of the earth" (Numbers 12:3).

In short, Moses was without question one of the greatest individuals in human history. Even so, Moses was subject to the same weakness as every individual in human history: death. The text of Deuteronomy states, "So Moses the servant of the LORD died there in the land of Moab, according to the word of the LORD" (34:5).

Although we often refuse to admit it, death is a part of life. Death is a part of who we are as human beings compromised by the corruption of sin. And yet, because of our salvation in Jesus Christ, we know that death is not the end. As John wrote in his gospel, "For God so loved the world that He gave His only begotten Son, that whoever believes in Him should not perish but have everlasting life" (3:16). Paul likewise observed, "'O Death, where is your sting? O Hades, where is your victory?' The sting of death is sin, and the strength of sin is the law. But thanks be to God, who gives us the victory through our Lord Jesus Christ" (1 Corinthians 15:55–57).

No matter who you are, and no matter what you've accomplished, death awaits. But for those who have repented and believed in the Lord Jesus Christ, death holds no fear. Rather, we can look forward to the end of this life with settled assurance of the blessings and glories that await in an eternity with Him.

REFLECTING ON THE TEXT

5) You know God is faithful, so how do you explain the evil and suffering in the world?

_____

_____

_____

_____

6) What are some specific ways that God has been faithful to you?

_____

_____

_____

_____

7) How would you defend the exclusivity of the God of the Bible?

_____

_____

_____

_____

_____

_____

8) Why can followers of Christ be free from the fear of death?

_____

_____

_____

_____

_____

PERSONAL RESPONSE

9) What are some of the ways God has been faithful to you despite your failings?

_____

_____

_____

_____

_____

_____

10) What are some ways you can express praise and worship to God this week because of His faithfulness in your life?

_____

_____

_____

_____

_____

_____

_____

12

REVIEWING KEY PRINCIPLES

DRAWING NEAR

What did you expect when you started your reading of Leviticus and Deuteronomy? How do those expectations compare with what you learned through the study of the text?

_____

_____

_____

_____

_____

_____

_____

THE CONTEXT

Leviticus and Deuteronomy are often thought of as "boring" books within the Bible. Many people (Christians included) avoid reading them because they expect to find nothing more significant than long lists of laws and drawn-out speeches. However, now that you have studied these books in greater detail, you have come to understand that the reality is far different. Both Leviticus and Deuteronomy are filled with poignant, powerful passages that are both edifying and uplifting.

Yes, Leviticus does contain a large number of laws. However, those laws, regulations, ordinances, and provisions are critical to understanding the character of God. In addition, the rituals and sacrifices prescribed in Leviticus offer a direct and visual window to the sacrifice of Jesus Christ. They help us gain a better understanding of critical doctrines such as holiness and atonement.

Likewise, some might be quick to dismiss Deuteronomy as a collection of historical and doctrinal speeches from the end of Moses' life. But such a dim view forfeits the insight Moses provides into the faithfulness and provision of God for His people. Few men who ever lived have enjoyed as intimate a relationship with God as Moses. His closing words in Deuteronomy give us unparalleled perspective on the Lord's love for His people and blessings we enjoy as His children.

Here are a few of the major principles we have found during our study. There are many more we don't have room to reiterate, so take some time to review the earlier studies—or, better still, to meditate on the passages of Scripture that we have covered. As you do, ask the Holy Spirit to give you wisdom and insight into His Word. He will not refuse.

EXPLORING THE MEANING

Sacrifice revealed the seriousness of sin. When modern readers of the Bible encounter the idea of sacrifice in the Old Testament, it is easy to process that concept in a purely academic sense—meaning, we have knowledge of what happened during these rituals: Families would gather at the tabernacle (and later at the temple) to offer a sacrifice either as a voluntary expression of worship or as a means of receiving forgiveness for sins. Yet the actual experience of offering a sacrifice would have been much more real and memorable.

Leviticus 1 gives us an overview of the process: "If his offering is a burnt sacrifice of the herd, let him offer a male without blemish; he shall offer it of his own free will at the door of the tabernacle of meeting before the LORD. Then he shall put his hand on the head of the burnt offering, and it will be accepted on his behalf to make atonement for him. He shall kill the bull before the LORD; and the priests, Aaron's sons, shall bring the blood and sprinkle the blood all around on the altar that is by the door of the tabernacle of meeting" (verses 3–5).

Imagine being a child and witnessing such a sacrifice. You see your father lead a lamb or bull to the entrance of the tabernacle. It is alive. It snorts and pulls against the rope that binds it. After a conversation with the priests, your father places his hand on the animal's head. You realize something significant is happening. With a quick motion, your father unsheathes a knife and cuts the animal's throat. You don't just see the blood, you smell it. You hear the sound it makes pooling on the ground. You watch as the priests begin dragging the now-lifeless carcass into the tabernacle compound, where it will be butchered and its pieces burned.

The message would be crystal clear. Sin is serious. Sin leads to death, because God is utterly righteous and perfectly just. And sin can only be covered over with blood.

God's standard of holiness is perfect. Leviticus 10 begins with a shocking moment: "Then Nadab and Abihu, the sons of Aaron, each took his censer and put fire in it, put incense on it, and offered profane fire before the LORD, which He had not commanded them. So fire went out from the LORD and devoured them, and they died before the LORD" (verses 1–2).

It is not immediately clear to the modern reader what these men did wrong. The "profane fire" may have been a sacrifice that was not included in God's specific instructions. Or the priests may have been drunk while performing their service at the altar (see verses 8–10). What is clear is that Nadab and Abihu violated God's standard of holiness. They had witnessed a miracle just moments before, in which God sent divine fire to consume their offerings (see 9:24). Yet they immediately dishonored God by bringing sin into His very presence— so that same divine fire ended their lives.

The deaths of Nadab and Abihu were similar to the fate of a man we read about later in the Bible, named Uzzah. King David wanted to bring the Ark of the Covenant into Jerusalem, so he had the ark placed on a cart and wheeled into the city—against God's clear prescriptions for the ark's transportation (Numbers 3:30–31; 4:15; Exodus 25:12–15). When the oxen driving the cart stumbled, Uzzah put his hand out and touched the ark to stabilize it. As a result, he was struck dead instantly (see 2 Samuel 6:6–8).

In both instances, people paid with their lives because they did not fear God as they ought or treat Him with the reverence He deserves and demands. How wonderful that we who belong to Christ in faith have received His perfect righteousness (Philippians 3:9), which is why we are able to come into God's presence without fear. That is an amazing gift of God's grace alone!

The Day of Atonement foreshadowed the atoning work of Christ. Leviticus 16 contains instructions for the Day of Atonement, which was to be observed each year by God's people. The purpose of this day was both simple and profound: "For on that day the priest shall make atonement for you, to cleanse you, that you may be clean from all your sins before the LORD" (verse 30).

The ceremony for the Day of Atonement is rich and filled with powerful imagery. The high priest's duties on that day foreshadowed Jesus' sacrifice on the cross. For example, only the high priest was allowed to enter the inner portion of the tabernacle, commonly called the Holy of Holies. But to do so, the priest was required to work through a staggering list of bathings, cleansings, and sacrifices, simply to walk through the door into the Most Holy place. This served as both a picture of and a contrast to Jesus, who as the perfect High Priest is the only one able to make atonement for sin, yet who has continual and unfettered access to the throne room of heaven because He Himself is God.

The Day of Atonement also involved two goats, whose respective fates were determined by God through casting lots (verse 8). The first goat was sacrificed within the tabernacle: "He shall kill the goat of the sin offering, which is for the people, bring its blood inside the veil . . . and sprinkle it on the mercy seat and before the mercy seat. So he shall make atonement . . . because of the uncleanness of the children of Israel, and because of their transgressions, for all their sins" (verses 15–16). The second goat was brought alive into the courtyard of the tabernacle. What happened next is a poignant visual: "Aaron shall lay both his hands on the head of the live goat, confess over it all the iniquities of the children of Israel, and all their transgressions, concerning all their sins, putting them on the head of the goat, and shall send it away into the wilderness . . . . The goat shall bear on itself all their iniquities to an uninhabited land" (verses 21–22). Like these goats, Jesus was killed on the mountain of God to make atonement for sin, and He carried away our sins on His body at the moment of His death. But unlike the Day of Atonement, Jesus' sacrifice made atonement once for all.

Israel's feasts show the importance of remembering God's faithfulness. "And the LORD spoke to Moses, saying, 'Speak to the children of Israel, and say to them: "The feasts of the LORD, which you shall proclaim to be holy convocations, these are My feasts"'" (Leviticus 23:1–2). Feasts, get-togethers, and other celebrations have been a common element of religious gatherings for thousands of years. Yet it's interesting to see the importance God placed on Israel coming together as a community several times a year to commemorate specific feasts.

The first of these celebrations was the Sabbath: "Six days shall work be done, but the seventh day is a Sabbath of solemn rest, a holy convocation" (verse 3). God was adamant that His people set aside one day each week for rest and worship. Another was the Passover and the Feast of Unleavened Bread, during which the Israelites were to remember God's miraculous provision during the Exodus from Egypt (see also Exodus 12:1–14). Another was the Day of Atonement, described in Leviticus 16. Still another was the Feast of Tabernacles, which was a week-long celebration of God's provision for Israel while they wandered in the wilderness.

The goal of these feasts and celebrations was at least partly worship, for each was an opportunity to present specific offerings and sacrifices to God. Yet another element of these feasts was the importance of remembering the past. God wanted His people to remember and celebrate His faithfulness so that the generations to come would not forget His gracious protection and provision.

Sin always carries consequences. The first chapter of Deuteronomy is a reminder that sin is serious and always brings with it consequences. When the Israelites first encountered the promised land, they refused to take possession of it because they were afraid of its inhabitants. Then, after the Lord proclaimed that none of them would enter the land because of their disobedience, they decided to attack the people of Canaan on their own.

First the people had rebelled against God by not taking action. Then they rebelled against God by taking action that He had not sanctioned. Not surprisingly, the attack went badly: "And the LORD said to me, 'Tell them, "Do not go up nor fight, for I am not among you; lest you be defeated before your enemies."' So I spoke to you; yet you would not listen, but rebelled against the command of the LORD, and presumptuously went up into the mountain. And the Amorites who dwelt in that mountain came out against you and chased you as bees do, and drove you back from Seir to Hormah. Then you returned and wept before the LORD, but the LORD would not listen to your voice nor give ear to you" (verses 42–45).

Moses, especially, was not exempt from the consequences of his sin either. He disobeyed God in the wilderness of Kadesh by striking a rock to produce water, thus taking some of the glory for himself rather than God (see Numbers 20:1–13). As a result, God proclaimed that Moses would not enter the promised land. Instead, "Joshua the son of Nun, who stands before you, he shall go in there. Encourage him, for he shall cause Israel to inherit it" (Deuteronomy 1:38).

One spiritual principle that is clear throughout the Bible is that sin separates people from God. Yet it is important to note that while our sin always carries consequences, it does not determine our salvation. Moses was prevented from entering the promised land because of his disobedience—a critical consequence. However, he repented and was restored to a right relationship with God. Likewise, we will encounter consequences when we rebel against God, yet we can always turn to Him to receive forgiveness and the blessing of His presence.

Trust and obey. Much of what Moses communicated to the Israelites in Deuteronomy can be boiled down to one central idea: Trust God. The previous generation had failed to trust God because they were terrified by the size and strength of the Canaanites. Their fear was larger than their faith.

As you read through Moses' appeals in Deuteronomy, notice that he never addressed the reality of the Canaanites. He never said, "These are the specific ways that God will help you defeat your enemies." Instead, he simply exhorted the Israelites to trust that God *would* help them: "When the LORD your God brings you into the land which you go to possess, and has cast out many nations before you, the Hittites and the Girgashites and the Amorites and the Canaanites and the Perizzites and the Hivites and the Jebusites, seven nations greater and mightier than you, and when the LORD your God delivers them over to you, you shall conquer them and utterly destroy them. You shall make no covenant with them nor show mercy to them" (7:1–2).

In short, Moses set before the current generation of Israelites the same choice that had thwarted the previous generation: Trust God or trust yourselves. In addition, he reminded the people why they *should* trust God: because of His character. "For the LORD your God is God of gods and Lord of lords, the great God, mighty and awesome, who shows no partiality nor takes a bribe. He administers justice for the fatherless and the widow, and loves the stranger, giving him food and clothing" (10:17–18).

Moses added, "You shall fear the LORD your God; you shall serve Him, and to Him you shall hold fast, and take oaths in His name. He is your praise, and He is your God, who has done for you these great and awesome things which your eyes have seen" (verses 20–21). This is the God we serve today—the One who is utterly worthy of our trust.

God does not tolerate idolatry. In Deuteronomy 12, Moses offered thorough instructions for how the Israelites should worship God once they took possession of the promised land. But the first was most shocking: "You shall utterly destroy all the places where the nations which you shall dispossess served their gods, on the high mountains and on the hills and under every green tree. And you shall destroy their altars, break their sacred pillars, and burn their wooden images with fire; you shall cut down the carved images of their gods and destroy their names from that place. You shall not worship the LORD your God with such things" (verses 2–4).

Ancient peoples believed the gods inhabited specific locations—often the tops of mountains. Therefore, it was common for pagan cultures to set up sites of worship in such "high places" they connected to specific deities. Moses reminded the Israelites to have no connection to these pagan practices. He commanded Israel to utterly destroy these false places of worship. God has no tolerance for idolatry.

That is just as true today. Many believe they can worship God through means that are outside of His expressed will. For example, some try to earn God's favor by doing good works, or at least by doing more good things than bad. Others believe that holding to certain extrabiblical standards earns them righteousness, which is legalism. Others seek to incorporate rituals from other religions into their worship—including practices from different Eastern religions, such as Buddhism. Such syncretism results only in disaster because it directly violates God's command to worship nothing but Him and in no way but according to His prescription. He is Lord.

God is always faithful. Moses began the book of Deuteronomy by detailing the failure of Israel's past generations when they rebelled against God in refusing to obey Him by entering the promised land. Moses ended his contribution to Deuteronomy with a song that highlights that same theme. It is important to note that in both cases, Moses also pointedly called the Israelites' attention to God's contrasting faithfulness.

"He is the Rock, His work is perfect," Moses wrote, "for all His ways are justice, a God of truth and without injustice; righteous and upright is He" (32:4). Later, Moses encouraged his hearers to remember how God had selected Israel's forefathers and lifted them up: "He found him in a desert land and in the wasteland, a howling wilderness; He encircled him, He instructed him, He kept him as the apple of His eye. As an eagle stirs up its nest, hovers over its young, spreading out its wings, taking them up, carrying them on its wings, so the LORD alone led him, and there was no foreign god with him" (verses 10–12).

Despite Israel's many and repeated transgressions, God was faithful to them in all respects. He reached out to them, nourished them, and gave them opportunity after opportunity to repent and return to a right relationship with Him. He has always been, and will always be, faithful to His chosen ones.

UNLEASHING THE TEXT

1) When have you been most encouraged during this study? Why?

_____

_____

_____

_____

_____

2) What are some remaining questions you would like to have answered after completing this study?

_____

_____

_____

_____

_____

3) What emphasis have you placed on personal holiness? What spiritual disciplines might aid and increase your personal holiness?

_____

_____

_____

_____

_____

4) What have you learned about the importance of obeying God in your life after reading about the Israelites' spiritual failures?

_____

_____

_____

_____

PERSONAL RESPONSE

5) How would you describe your relationship with God? Would you say it is healthy and growing, or stunted and distant? Explain.

_____

_____

_____

_____

_____

_____

6) In what areas of your life have you been most convicted during this study? What exact things will you do to address these convictions? Be specific.

_____

_____

_____

_____

7) What have you learned about God's nature and character throughout this study?

_____

_____

_____

_____

8) In what areas do you hope to grow spiritually over the coming weeks and months? What steps will you need to take in order to achieve that growth?

_____

_____

_____

_____

_____

If you would like to continue in your study of the Old Testament, read the next title in this series: _2 Samuel: David's Heart Revealed._

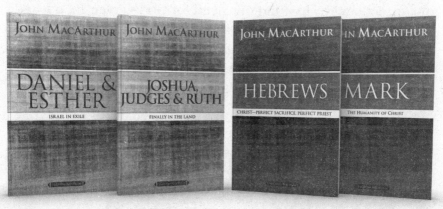

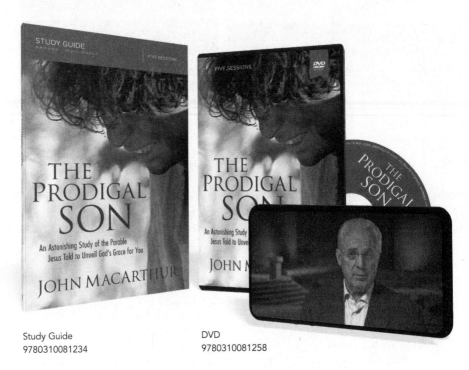

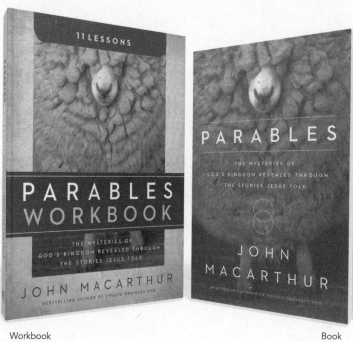